LADDER LEADERS

The Team

The Task

The Transition

Cover design by: Joe De Leon
Cover photo by: sirtravelalot

ISBN: 978-1-954089-24-2   1 2 3 4 5 6 7 8 9 10

Printed in the United States of America

LADDER LEADERS

The Team

The Task

The Transition

SAM CHAND

INSPIRE

CONTENTS

PART I

WHO'S HOLDING YOUR LADDER?

INTRODUCTION

I stared out the window while I waited for someone to call me into the sanctuary. I was a featured speaker at a conference at Evangel Church in Queens, New York. As I meditated on the points I wanted to cover, something in the street below diverted my attention.

A man stood on a ladder painting—not that uncommon a sight. I smiled, remembering my student days in Bible college. I had spent my summers doing that kind of work, and I couldn't take my eyes off the man. For several minutes I watched his graceful motions as he moved his brush across the surface.

"I wonder who's holding the ladder for him?" I asked aloud. I couldn't see all the way to the street level.

Although I couldn't see them, someone had to be down there bracing the painter's ladder. An impression was made while I stared down from about eight floors above street level. As I watched the man paint the exterior wall, I noticed he could cover only a limited area. He stretched as far as he could to the left and then to the right and even reached above his head. As I observed him, it occurred to me that he was only going to the height that he was comfortable in climbing or reaching.

What would allow him to go higher? I asked myself. I could see that he stood on an extension ladder so he could go higher—and he would have to if he wanted to finish the job. If the ladder reached the top of the building, he still needed one thing. He had to have someone on the street level hold his ladder steady while he worked.

By himself, the painter couldn't go any farther. He had stretched and reached and done everything he could by himself. He needed help. As I watched, I thought about how the painter's situation was an illustration of an important leadership principle. It struck me that, whether in management or systems, the effectiveness of a leader depends on the people who hold the ladder—those who are in support roles in the business, organization or church.

Then another thought struck me: *Those who hold the ladders are as important as the leaders themselves.*

My mind wouldn't let go of that image. As I stared out that window in Queens, I kept thinking, *No leader gets to the top without those down below who hold the ladder.* I craned my neck trying to see the street level, but I never could see who held that ladder.

Then I smiled as my mind shifted to the symbolism of leadership, success and people in enabling roles. Those who faithfully support from the bottom are often unseen, but that doesn't diminish their importance or the need for them. Sometimes God may be the only One who knows who's holding the ladder.

I took the idea even further. I began to think of the ladder as the symbol of the dream—the vision of the leader—and the painter as the visionary. Once the visionary begins climbing her ladder, the scope of her leadership can be wide and far-reaching or narrow and confined. Which of those two stories emerges depends on the quality of the team of ladder holders the leader recruits and develops.

A painter on a ladder could have all the training and expertise possible, the most expensive equipment, years of experience and knowledge about his trade—and be extremely passionate about what he is doing. But that's not the deciding factor. The ladder holders determine the height of the painter.

"That's it!" I cried out. "Those who hold the ladder control the ascent of the visionaries."

As we will explore in Part I of this book, the discovery, development and deployment of a team of ladder holders forms the foundation of a leader's journey toward fulfilling his vision. Some may think the image of "ladder holders" suggests arrogance. After all, the leader is leveraging the strength and abilities of others to realize his own dreams.

In fact, I would argue that the idea that a leader can accomplish the vision *without* the help of a valued team implies far more arrogance! The recruitment of ladder holders is not exploitation, but development of people—many of whom will go on to ascend ladders of their own. Being a ladder holder is an important step in each of our journeys as ladder climbers. All of us are both ladder climbers and ladder holders.

If you haven't noticed, while the ladder serves as an illustration of the need to develop a team to support our visions as leaders, it also serves as a metaphor for the journey of leadership itself. Each rung represents challenges that we must face and skills we must develop before we can ascend in influence and impact. In Part II of this book, I will address these core competencies. Each one could be explored in a book of its own, but I offer them as launchpads for self-assessment and further study.

Finally, the ladder serves as a meaningful symbol of transition. After all, ladders have a finite number of rungs, and those who climb them eventually reach a destination, if they continue to ascend. Over the course of our leadership journeys, we may find ourself on more than one ladder.

According to a recent study from the Bureau of Labor Statistics, the average person will hold twelve jobs in the course of his or her career. While some of these will be promotions within a single career, others will find themselves pursuing—or being placed in—positions that may be far removed from what the trajectory of their lives would have suggested. Transitions such as these require grace, flexibility and a willingness to risk failure. In Part III of this book, I will share my personal experience with transition and the lessons I learned along the way.

Close behind the choice of ladder holders, perhaps the most mean-ingful choices we face are what we leave behind. Legacy is *whom* we will leave behind. Inheritance is *what* we will leave behind. There is the organization over which we are given stewardship, the people we have been tasked with developing, the systems that will allow for complexity and scale. These will all survive our tenures on the various ladders we climb. Their effectiveness—or dysfunction—will serve as a testimony to our leadership, whether for good or for ill.

The challenge of leadership is simultaneous attention to all three of these broad areas. For example, transition may come at any time in our journeys, and it usually doesn't wait for our permission to occur. Likewise, the development of ladder holders is not something that we accomplish once and then abandon—it is an iterative and con-tinuous process that requires more or less attention, depending on where we are in our careers. Finally, we begin shaping our legacy from the point we ascend the first rung of our leadership ladders. It takes immense focus and determination to address all three aspects of "ladder leadership."

My hope and prayer are that this book will stimulate self-reflection and provide tools for strengthening our grip on the ladders each of us climbs. Whatever rung we may currently be standing on, it's never too late—or too early—to approach our leadership journeys with a fresh set of eyes.

CHAPTER 1
DISCOVER

People are not your most important asset. The right people are.
—Jim Collins, researcher and author

I'm a nobody."

"I don't make any difference. No one even misses me when I'm absent."

"I just answer the telephone in our office and do a little word processing. Anybody can do what I do."

"I'm not a preacher or a singer, so I'm just one of the lesser lights in our church."

Those are typical of the kinds of responses I've heard from individuals—the support people—those who are just as important in their own supporting roles as the stars of the show.

I want to be clear about discovering ladder holders:

- They are the foundation of our organizations.

- They are the ones who allow us to reach our highest potential.

- They hold the ladder so securely that we don't have to fret or constantly worry if we'll fall.

If the fulfillment of our vision is dependent not only on our own commitment and competence, but on that of the teams that we gather around us, could there be a more crucial task than discovering, developing and deploying those ladder holders? After all, they may determine the difference between our success and failure.

BAD INGREDIENTS

Let's look more closely at those we choose to hold our ladders. We can't just throw anybody into the job. I've found that it is helpful not only to identify the qualities I am looking for, but also the characteristics that are red flags in the selection process. To get started, here are the kinds of people we *don't* want to hold our ladders.

Undependable

Sometimes you're so tired of reminding people to take up their positions at the foot of the ladder that you try to mount the steps by yourself without any support. I'll take an unskilled, dependable ladder holder any day over a skilled, undependable one. At least one of them can be trained.

Casual

Are the people you hire or recruit intentional about their work, or are they casual and distracted in their approach? Will your ladder holder curl all his toes around the bottom rungs and hold the ladder with both hands? Or will he have one hand draped casually across one of the rungs and a cup of Starbucks coffee in the other?

Conditional

These are the resumé builders. They are committed to holding your ladder as long as an opportunity to hold a larger, more prestigious ladder doesn't present itself. Their commitment is not to you and your vision, but to the advancement of their own careers. If you're not careful, they'll move on to another ladder, and you'll be stuck forty feet in the air.

Unhappy

Whether it's the disgruntled employee or the church attendee who's been coming for years but can't stand the music and constantly complains about the preaching, unhappy people don't usually change, even when the circumstances do. Not to mention, their misery is contagious.

Puppets

"Yes" men and women may be initially supportive, but they ultimately make unreliable ladder holders when you need them most—to tell you the truth when the truth may be uncomfortable for you to hear.

THE RIGHT STUFF

Since we've identified what *not* to look for in ladder holders, what core qualities should we seek instead? There are five qualities I'd insist on, and there are others I'd like to see and that I would hope for. These are the essentials for ladder holders.

Strength

They must be people who can handle instruction and criticism, with whom you can use plain language and not have to walk on eggshells, withhold feedback and then fix things for them. If they need to be corrected in certain areas, they can change without you having to worry about how much you're going to hurt their feelings. You must have people holding the ladder who can handle instructions in two to three words and be able to follow through quickly.

Attentiveness

They need to be able to pay attention—alert to what you're saying and absorbing it quickly. You don't want to give them the same lessons repeatedly. Attentive people understand the first time.

Faithfulness

I'm not referring to having faith in the Lord. I'm talking about having faith in you as their leader and being committed to you. You need people who remain at the ladder no matter how difficult things become. As long as you're up there, the faithful show you that you can be assured they are still down below. They don't need you constantly yelling down, "You're doing a great job. You're wonderful." They're steady, and you can count on them.

Firmness

By this I mean that they cannot be exploited by manipulative people. In every church and organization there are manipulative types. They may be extremely self-deceived or just mean-spirited. It doesn't matter which because the end is the same. They want to destroy the present plans and operations or build a name for themselves. Ladder holders need to be strong enough to discern their tactics and stand up to them.

Loyalty

I do not mean they must agree with you all the time. Loyalty doesn't mean repeating, "Yes, yes, yes," no matter what the visionary says. They may disagree with your *head* but not your *heart*. They may disagree with *how* you do things but not *why* you do things. They may disagree with your *methods* but not your *motivations*.

WHO VS. WHAT

You may have noticed in the above characteristics the absence of specific skills or competencies. This is not because I'm suggesting we recruit incompetent or unskilled people as ladder holders. However, from my experience as a CEO with paid employees, I learned that you hire people for *what* they know; you fire them for *who* they are. In other words, if we pay more attention to why we fire people and let that influence whom we hire, we will end up needing to fire fewer people.

A pastor may hire the musician because she can make the simplest music sound like a concerto in every piece she plays. He fires her because she has a bad attitude. A CEO may hire an office manager because he is a computer whiz and understands spreadsheets, profit and loss, government regulations and knows all the latest software. He fires him because he can't get along with people.

Randall Murphy, the founder and president of the Acclivus Corporation, once said, "When you are assigned the task of taking the hill—or the market—you are less concerned about who is *for* you and more concerned about who is *with* you."

Just because people say, "I'm for you," that isn't the real issue. The real issue is what they do. Do they do what they promise? Do they faithfully follow their words by their actions? These are the characteristics we should look for in ladder holders. With them holding our ladders, we can scale them with confidence, focusing on the things that really matter.

THE RECRUIT'S ADVANTAGE

Continuing with the ladder metaphor, if you were to need someone to hold a forty-foot ladder, would you post the job in the classified ads or start recruiting among trusted people you already knew?

Whether the position is paid or unpaid, those who volunteer are likely to be less experienced than the team members we recruit. The wrong people are often the first ones to volunteer—possibly, because they have nothing else to do. How does a volunteer get "unvolunteered" if the situation doesn't work out? The most qualified people are busy and engaged elsewhere. They won't come along unless someone recruits them.

The best Sunday school teacher may not be the one who offers to do it. The person for the job might be the public school teacher who doesn't think she wants to spend another day with kids. However, if a leader takes time to share the vision for Sunday school, and she can see there is support from the top down, it's possible to change her mind.

When Jesus needed disciples, He didn't wait around to see who would volunteer. Instead, He went out and chose the men He wanted. That should be your goal when hiring people. When seeking the proper person to fill a job, the resume can't help you make this kind of decision; the Holy Spirit must draw you to the right candidate, sometimes even in spite of the resume.

When choosing people for your team, remember the acrostic ASK. Unlike people who volunteer, ASK candidates are recruited because of their *attitudes, skills* and *knowledge,* the three qualities needed for players on a winning team.

Attitude

When you hire people with the right attitude, you can teach them to do anything. A good attitude can help a person conquer the most difficult circumstances. Employees with good attitudes work hard, are driven to reach goals and continue to press on regardless of the roadblocks. People with bad attitudes are unmotivated, negative and self-absorbed. No matter how talented they are, they never amount to much.

Skill

Skill is relative and is determined by the amount of competence needed for the task at hand. While some skills can be developed and refined on the job, you need to identify the baseline competence needed to accomplish the task without slowing progress or adding work to other teammates who may need to compensate for an unskilled colleague.

Knowledge

The person who has a great attitude, superb skills, and also extensive knowledge is the ideal employee or team member. Those with skill and knowledge can fix what is broken and explain why it broke in the first place. But knowledge without skill is like a doctor who can make a diagnosis but doesn't know how to treat the illness.

Candidates with the right balance of ASK need to be asked what they want to do. If they are forced into jobs that don't suit their temperaments and passions, they won't be fully productive. People are most productive when they are passionate about what they are doing. Always try to put people into positions they care about. Of course, the only way to do that is to know them and understand their passions.

I realize that there are certain positions that need to be filled and certain tasks and portfolios that need to be taken care of. I'm not suggesting that we hire people for jobs we don't need done. However, I am recommending a bias toward recruiting good people, understanding their skills and passions, then finding ways they can be leveraged toward accomplishing your organization's mission and vision.

HIRING AND FIRING

What do you do when it's time to put someone on staff? My suggestion is that you need to re-think your policy. You want competent people, obviously. But when you select ladder holders, you need to spend more time examining who they are rather than what they know.

You can read their resumés, and you can talk to people they've worked for and with. That is important. But troubles in the job usually start over personality issues and not over competency. Once hired, they will give you joy or grief. With few exceptions, the people I have fired I have terminated because of their attitudes. Rarely have I needed to get rid of someone for lack of ability to do the job.

With that in mind, I recommend following this rule: *Hire slowly and fire quickly.*

It's better to have a vacancy than to have bad help. Suppose the doctor diagnoses you with cancer, says surgery is the only option and asks, "When would you want it scheduled?" I'm guessing you'll say, "As soon as possible."

As a leader, a good question to ask yourself is this: *Why do I tolerate incompetent staff? Why do I allow disgruntled team members to infect the rest of the staff with their bad attitudes?*

Simply put, don't rush hiring decisions; don't delay firing decisions.

The best time to fire somebody is the first time it goes through your head. We tend to get our roles confused again here. Instead of thinking as a CEO and for the good of the organization, we tend to switch to a pastoral role and figure out ways to excuse or overlook problems serious enough that we'd consider terminating them.

I've also learned that if the situation is serious enough to fire people and I don't, I soon begin to search for reasons to keep them.

The bias toward recruiting that I am advocating may require not only adding fresh people to your team of ladder holders, but rearranging existing people into roles and responsibilities that are better aligned with their skills and passions. Making these important shifts can inspire your team and can help the entire organization function better. In fact, they may help the team rise to a level they previously couldn't reach.

Ultimately, seeking recruits versus volunteers may not give you all the ladder holders you need. However, it will create a culture that places emphasis on the skills and attitudes that you value, and that culture will attract like-minded people to join your team, allowing you to climb higher than you would have with just a group of volunteers.

CHAPTER 2
DEVELOP

The only thing worse than training your employees and having
them leave is not training them and having them stay.
—Henry Ford, inventor and entrepreneur

It is rare that a team of ladder holders arrives on the scene ready to help you carry out your vision. That is where the task of development comes in. While many ladder holders may already be trained to do a job, our ultimate goal is to develop them as people. In this chapter, I will not have the time to address every detail surrounding leadership development, but I hope to make some key distinctions, lay out some principles and give a roadmap for deeper reflection and success as we build our teams.

DEVELOPMENT VS. TRAINING
First, there is a vast difference between training people for a specific duty and developing them as leaders. Training focuses on tasks; developing focuses on the person. Training is unidirectional; developing

is omni-directional. We train people to become receptionists. When you're finished, they're good receptionists, and they do their tasks well. However, we have not developed them so that they are ready to move into other positions. If we don't develop and equip others, we're never going to have the kind of ladder holders we need—especially when we want to climb to the highest rungs.

Developing leaders isn't an endgame in which leaders only become effective when they are fully actualized. Instead, time spent developing leaders returns itself as the quality of leadership is raised across the organization. More importantly, mentoring others also helps us as leaders to grow.

We determine the ceiling for the leaders who work for us. If you become a better leader, the entire organization rises with you. Not only should we develop the leaders under us, but we should encourage them to seek outside mentors who can also develop them in ways that we cannot. Leaders should have multiple people developing them.

People often say, "He is a born leader." I respectfully disagree. Leaders aren't born; they're made, like bread is made. Leadership development is an intentional activity. Raisin bread doesn't appear by itself even if we leave the ingredients on the kitchen counter overnight. Someone must consciously take ingredients and knead them together, put the mixture under the right amount of heat and allow it to rise, then punch it down and start over again until the dough is the perfect consistency. Only then will it rise above the pan. Helping a leader rise takes this same kind of intentional activity.

THE RAW MATERIALS

I believe everyone has the ingredients needed to be a leader. We are all leaders at different times and places—whether in our families, churches or workplaces. So, if everyone is capable of being a leader, how do we explain the difference in ability among leaders?

If we could measure people on a leadership scale of one to ten, some people will only rise to a level three while others will rise to a ten. The ingredients are there, but they never seem to come together to their full potential. That's where we come in. What can our leaders accomplish if we invest time in developing them?

Three key ingredients, when properly combined, affect leadership development. The first is the raw material itself. An individual's intelligence, physical and emotional health, energy level, and personality will all play a part in the kind of leader they become.

The second is the context in which they are developed. Some leaders develop better through quiet, one-on-one coaching. Other leaders learn through trial and error, working through demanding leadership challenges while being encouraged from the sidelines.

The third ingredient is the person doing the development. Ultimately, a mentor can only teach what he or she already knows.

Just like the contestants in a cooking show are given a limited number of ingredients, the result of leadership development is determined by how the mentor uses the ingredients in a given context. A shy leader may need quiet, supportive coaching. If he is trained by a mentor who believes in trial-by-fire, the leader won't grow much. Likewise, if the developing leader thrives on challenges but doesn't have hands-on opportunities to practice his new skills, he will not reach his full potential.

Developing and mentoring leaders is like teaching babies to walk. First, the parents help them stand on their own without falling down. Once the baby has mastered standing, the parents move a few feet away and encourage the baby to take a step. Eventually, the parents move across the room and entice the baby to come to them. If the baby gets started in the wrong direction, the parents turn her around. When it appears the baby might run into obstacles, parents rush to protect her. And, of course, a good parent always picks the baby up when she falls and helps her start over again.

It takes time for babies to learn to walk, and it takes time for leaders to develop their skills. It is a learning process that continues. There is no such thing as a fully developed leader. It's a myth.

THE POWER OF MENTORING

I sometimes call myself an accidental leader. Until recently, I was never mentored, so mentoring others didn't come easy to me. As a result, the mentoring I did was also accidental. I thought mentoring others meant recommending good management books I had read. I didn't intentionally create leaders; consequently, when I saw leaders rise on their own, I didn't know what to do with them. In some cases,

I felt threatened by their potential, so I did stupid things to diminish their engagement. As a result, we all became dysfunctional.

I've matured through those experiences and now know that I had to grow personally before I could successfully mentor others. One of the keys to my own growth was surrounding myself with people who are better than I am. Sometimes new leaders find doing so intimidating; they're afraid their candles won't shine as brightly in a room full of bonfires. They prefer to stay in the dark where they have the only light shining. But the truth is that you don't know it all, and you shouldn't be afraid to ask for help. Understanding your own inadequacies means you're less likely to pass them on. Learning from those who are more experienced and being humbled by your own limitations can help you develop and more fully develop others.

At this time, I have eleven mentors who each speak to me about a different area of my life. How did I find these mentors?

- I categorized each area of my life that needed ongoing mentoring and coaching.

- I identified people with specialized knowledge and skill in those areas.

- I asked them.

So, what is mentoring? John C. Crosby, executive director of The Uncommon Individual Foundation, an organization devoted exclusively to mentoring, said, "Mentoring is a brain to pick, an ear to listen, and a push in the right direction." In his book *The Kindness of Strangers,* Marc Freedman wrote, "Mentoring is mostly about small victories and subtle changes." They're right. Mentoring isn't about the big things; it is about the small ones.

I believe that developing a leader begins by spending time with her. Does she know what her gifts are? Is she using them? If not, help her to develop both the understanding and practice of her unique gifts. Doing so can help you establish trust as she sees that you're not trying to change her, you're only trying to make her a better version of who she already is.

FROM THE INSIDE OUT

As Jennifer Schuchmann writes in her book, *Your Unforgettable Life*, "Do the vice presidents at Ford Motor Company think of themselves as 'car guys'? Do the leaders at Unilever think of themselves as 'soap makers'? Do the executives at Walmart think of themselves as 'retail specialists'?"

No. When executives reach a certain level of leadership, it is no longer about managing the product or service. It is about leading people. If the executives at these companies depended on their ability to make cars, manufacture soap and sell toiletries, they wouldn't be defined as great leaders. True leadership has to do with managing people and ideas. That's why good leaders can easily transition from company to company or even industry to industry. Their talents aren't demonstrated in their products; they're demonstrated in their people.

That's why I'm encouraging us to embrace our responsibility to *develop* leaders strategically and spiritually. When developing others, we need to spend as much time on the internal life, as we do on the parts you can see. Leadership is a matter of how to *be*, not how to *do*. This is the *who*, not the *what*.

We need to prepare the leaders we develop. They have to be cultivated at a personal level. If we don't take the time to make sure the individual is ready, our mentoring will be for naught. But if we take the time to properly prepare people, then our mentoring will help them change from the inside out.

Leaders must understand that to truly develop, they must first work on themselves; only then can they focus on others. Working on self includes all the touchy-feely things on the inside of who they are. It also includes basic things about their jobs, such as getting the work done, holding their people accountable for what they do and staying focused. Once they've gotten a handle on self, they can move to focusing on others—working toward gaining commitment from their team, managing conflict and overcoming obstacles.

Perhaps the best way to see progress in the people you are mentoring is when you notice they are mentoring other people. They've moved from leading projects to managing people. Not everyone you try to develop will make this transition. Some will try and fail and never try again. But when we see that leader finally take ownership over developing another leader, we might actually see the roof rise to meet the capacity of our growing team of ladder holders.

CHAPTER 3

DEPLOY

No person can be a great leader unless he takes genuine
joy in the successes of those under him.
—W. H. Auden, poet and author

The process of developing and then deploying ladder holders can sometimes feel threatening. Why? If we're doing it right, we will be preparing people now who can step in and fill our jobs at any time. These fears are based on the misconception that ignoring the need for a successor somehow grants a leader job security. *What if the people I train become more successful than me?* we may wonder. *What if they are better at doing my job than I am?*

EXPANSION STRATEGY

These fears are natural, but we have to set them aside. Eventually the ceiling will rise, and we should be the one to lift it. Having additional leaders at the top of the ladder can help to raise the roof beams. Think how much an organization could grow if there were two at the top.

What if there were four or maybe even sixteen top leaders? Equipping leaders to do what you do doesn't have to be an exit strategy; it can be an expansion strategy.

An orchestra director who leads hundreds of professional musicians was asked, "What is the hardest instrument to play?" He didn't hesitate in his reply. "Second fiddle. Anybody can play first chair, but playing second chair is much more difficult."

This makes sense. Those in the second seat are often doing the same type and amount of work as those in the first chair. In some instances, they may be doing more, if they run interference by keeping people away from the top position. They get less recognition and less compensation; and should a string break, they must be willing to pass their instruments over to the first chair players.

When the first chair leaves, the second chair must also overcome the stereotypes and rumors that she wasn't good enough to be there in the first place and still find a way to do her job. Helping those in the second chair be prepared shouldn't be threatening, it should be an honor.

When our terms end, we can leave behind three things. The first is memories. The second is a well-developed leader. The third, and perhaps most important, is a roof that is higher than when we came in.

FROM CLIMBERS TO HOLDERS

In reading what I've written so far, you may assume that if you're a leader, all you need to do is concentrate on and develop other ladder holders. That's only half the concept.

Here's the other half: Every true disciple of Jesus Christ holds somebody's ladder. That's God's plan. We need each other, and we fulfill God's plan when we hold others' ladders.

We tend to forget that those of us who are leaders are ladder climbers and also ladder holders. Furthermore, we'll always be ladder holders, even if we're high-stepping climbers. Effective leaders understand that they are holding someone's ladder, whether it's the business partner's ladder, that of another pastor or a like-minded organizational leader. God has called all of us to hold ladders for others.

Effective leaders recognize two facts:

1) In leadership we will always need ladder holders.

2) In leadership we will also hold someone else's ladder. We are meant to support, assist and help others in their climb upward.

Another way to get to this is to ask yourself, *What kind of ladder holder would I like?* If you want to develop superior ladder holders, you need to become a superior ladder holder yourself. If you are a leader, here's my challenge to you: Whose ladder can you hold? What business leader can you mentor? Instead of looking at potential recruits and asking, "How can they serve me?" ask, "How can I serve them?"

God always intended for service to be a street on which we travel both ways. It is the law of reciprocity, and it teaches us that what we give will come back to us. That's absolutely true; however, the problem is that we can only give what we have. We can only pass on what we possess. If we aren't good ladder holders, how can we expect to have good ladder holders helping us?

It makes me think of the law of tithing in the Old Testament. God required all faithful Jews to give ten percent of their income to support the priests (hold their ladders). That's not the end of the law. The priests then gave ten percent to support the high priest. Even the priests had ladders to hold. That's always God's way of working.

If each of us is able to acknowledge the principle, it means that although we're leaders, we're also ladder holders. Here are a few more questions for you to ponder:

- Do I possess those five essential qualities of good ladder holders?

- Do I intentionally hold someone else's ladder?

- Am I a dependable ladder holder?

- When was the last time I walked past a visionary leader and said, "I really like her vision and like where she's going. I want to work alongside her and assist her by holding her ladder"?

- When was the last time I asked, "What leader can I help?" (Too often we are only looking for people to help us.)

What does it say about me if I always seek someone to hold my ladder, but I'm unwilling to hold another person's ladder? There's an old saying that most preachers will travel to the other corner of the world to preach a sermon, but they won't cross the street to hear one. Is that true of you? Here are other questions to ask yourself:

- When was the last time I attended a leadership conference when I wasn't a speaker?

- When did I go to a conference just to hear somebody else?

- When was the last time I read a book and thought, *I really like this*, and then corresponded with the author?

- When was the last time I saw somebody else's advertisement in a magazine and said, "I want to serve that person"?

It's the principle, which is also in the Bible, that we reap what we sow. If you sow holding ladders, you reap those who will hold your ladder. We receive by giving. This is just as true with ladder holding as anything else. It's not easy for many of us in leadership to be ladder holders.

THE INTENTIONAL MENTOR

I still remember the question my friend, Tom Fortson, asked me. Tom, who was at the time executive vice president of Promise Keepers, visited our college one day, and I gave him a tour around the college. On the steps of our chapel he paused and asked, "Can you tell me when you became a leader?"

"No, I really can't," I said. Immediately my mind flashed back to something John Maxwell once told me about himself. If Tom Fortson had asked John when he became a leader, John would have known how to answer. For him, that defining moment happened during his elementary school days. The class planned a mock courtroom. The students chose the jury, the defendant, the defense attorney, and the prosecutor. The class elected John the judge. Because of their confidence in his ability, on that day, John knew he was going to become a leader.

I told that story to Tom Fortson and added, "I haven't had that kind of epiphany in my life. I've just been one of those to whom leadership was slowly revealed."

Tom's question has stayed with me, and I've thought about it many times. When I speak in churches, I discover that most of the senior pastors are also accidental leaders. It's just as true when I ask about leadership in the marketplace.

I can't recall a single instance during my time in Bible college, seminary or denominational experience when anyone pointed out my leadership ability. Not once has a single person ever said to me, "I see potential in you. Good things are going to happen in your life. Could I walk with you? May I hold your ladder?"

Fine individuals have given me excellent advice; others have opened doors for me. No one has walked with me as my ladder holder. The realization that no one openly and intentionally mentored me has caused me to become more intentional to mentor others. That's my way of holding ladders.

For some people, that ability flows freely and they simply do it. Because the ability comes naturally, they rarely think much about it. Others like me don't find it easy because we have no role models to guide us. Because I was never intentionally mentored, I don't know the tracks to run on. I'm an accidental leader, but I don't want to be an accidental mentor.

Here are some large and final questions:

- Whose ladder are you holding right now?

- Who is climbing upward and trusting you to be there at the bottom, bracing the ladder for him or her?

- Who is climbing high because you stepped out of the way and said, "Let me support you"?

- Who will look back one day and say, "I rose forty-five feet in the air because you held my ladder"?

We have opportunities to be somebody's ladder holder. Because no one has done it for us, it may be difficult to intentionally commit ourselves to holding ladders, but it's not impossible. And it doesn't excuse us. It only means that it may take a little more effort for us accidental leaders to become intentional servants. But we can do it. We can commit ourselves to learning how to hold the ladders so others can climb high and some of them may even soar above us.

Nobody ever climbed Mt. Everest without a team. People climb Stone Mountain outside Atlanta because it's a relatively easy path and they don't need a team. No matter how high we go we should be holding somebody else's ladder—that's God's plan.

As leaders, when we start upward, our most important decision is to choose the right ladder holders; as ladder holders, our most important decision is to select which ladders we hold.

Here's one way I like to think of it. When we accomplish great things on our own ladder, we remember what we've done. When we intentionally hold others' ladders and they accomplish great things, they remember us. Their achievements become our legacy.

MASTERING THE RUNGS

INTRODUCTION

Now that we are discovering, developing and deploying our ladder holders, it is time to begin the climb. In Part II of this book, I will identify ten core competencies that leaders must develop in themselves as they scale the ladder and accomplish their vision.

A key factor in succeeding in these competencies has nothing to do with competence, but something far deeper. Professor and author Joseph Campbell once said, "There is perhaps nothing worse than reaching the top of the ladder and discovering that you're on the wrong wall." He meant that too many people take what he called the prudent path in life; therefore they miss the joy of being a part of something that really matters. Before you start climbing, you have to do two things:

3) *You need to decide where you want to go.* Why are you on the ladder in the first place? What tools do you need while you're climbing the ladder? What tools will you need when you reach the top? One thing I learned during my student days when I painted was that it was just too tiring and time consuming to go up and down that ladder. I had to make sure I had everything ready before I started up.

4) *You need to be clear about your vision.* You need to be able to tell your ladder holders why you're up there and what you're working toward. As you get higher on the ladder and it sways, you had better be sure you know why you're there. When you go through those turbulent times—and we all do—you'd better be clear about your reason for being so high off the ground.

In other words, leaders must first define the *what*—that which they want done. Once they know that answer, they need to be clear on *why*. The *why* is the motivation for the *what*, and it runs much deeper than the *what* and sustains you through the inevitable challenges that you will face in your leadership journey.

At the age of forty-four, I finally discovered who I was and what I was called to do: to help others succeed. I love doing leadership development, and it feeds my passion. It brings me fulfillment at a deeper level. As clearly as I perceive who I am, it is just as clear who I am not and what I don't want to do. I am someone who is motivated by the opportunity to develop leaders.

As I've grappled with leadership development, it occurred to me that we talk a lot about near-death experiences. I'm convinced that most people have what I call near-life experiences. They come close to being fully alive but never discover who they really are. They never work passionately at the things they're good at doing. Until you discover who you are, you won't climb the steps of the ladder that God wants you to climb.

These "bottom-rung" questions to ask yourself include:

- What am I passionate about?

- What are my gifts and talents?

- To what kind of work is God calling me?

- What frustrates me?

- What makes me cry?

- What brings me joy?

If you can tune into those things, those existential concepts in life, you're going to get the best results as you ascend the leadership ladder.

In addition to identifying your core motivations, you must dedicate focused effort to *skill formation*. Most of the leaders of my generation—the boomer generation—are *accidental leaders*. We stumbled into leadership. I don't remember anybody ever saying to me, "Sam, I see some potential in you."

People sent me signals, but no one said, "I'd like to walk this journey with you. You don't have to call me mentor. Here's my phone number. Call me any time. In fact, if you don't mind, may I keep tabs with you and watch how you're doing?"

I wish someone had done that; so do many other accidental leaders.

Here's the challenge. You can only give what you have. You can't pass on what you don't possess, because you tend to teach the way you were taught. Are you going to inflict the same accidental leadership on the next generation? Or are you going to have a plan?

When I consult with church leaders or business executives, I've found the same challenges are common to all leaders. Regardless of whether you are leading a small church or a Fortune 500 company, there are ten common challenges all leaders share. We're going to look at each one in detail.

As president of a college, I tackled these same ten challenges. Each time I confronted them I thought, *I am the only one who has ever had to face this before.* But now, as a leadership consultant, I talk to thousands of leaders each year; and I've learned that leaders have more in common than we have separating us.

You're not the only one who is facing these hurdles. You can learn to recognize patterns of failure and success from those who've faced similar circumstances. These challenges aren't a phase you go through once and never return. You don't learn how to handle a challenge once and then never face it again. Instead, you will continue to face the same obstacles throughout your personal and professional life.

Think about it. How many of us have said, "If I could just get organized"? The implicit thought is that if we do it once we will never have to do it again. That's not true. We may temporarily control the clutter; but as we take on additional responsibility, additional clutter comes with it. Whether that clutter is in our office (additional paperwork), our time (additional meetings), or our mind (lack of focus), the challenge will continue to reoccur.

The ten challenges presented in this part of the book are not like a rock in the middle of the highway that you go around once and never come back to. If you're having problems dealing with a two-million-dollar budget, imagine what it will be like to manage a fifty-million-dollar budget. If you have challenges with a staff of five, think about the challenges you'll have with a staff of 157. No, these challenges aren't rocks you go around; these are challenges that will continue to rock your world. The higher you go on the ladder, the more the reverberations will shake the ladder from the bottom to the top.

As a leader, it is your job to learn how to hold on to the ladder even when it is being shaken. It is also your responsibility to figure out how you can prevent or minimize shaking in the future. Can you reduce the reverberations? Can you stop the top of the ladder from swaying? Can you secure the bottom better?

Understanding these challenges will help you to secure your founda-
tions. The challenges will continually shake your ladder, but you can
learn how to hang on while it sways, anticipate when it is coming
your way and keep it from shaking all day.

CHAPTER 4
FOCUS

Focus is reflected in the capacity to identify and devote the majority
of your time and energy to the "critical few" objectives and issues,
while still managing to deal with the "important many."
—Sam T. Manoogian, independent leadership consultant

As leaders, we often have so many opportunities before us that it's hard to focus on only one. This dilemma isn't unique to pastors or churches. Business leaders also face the same struggle when adding new products and services, changing their marketing approach, or evaluating opportunities to expand. When presented with overwhelming choices, how do we focus on the "critical few" while still managing to deal with the "important many"?

Finding focus is not difficult;

Keeping focus is.

As president of a college, people always wanted to give me a new focus. They would come to me with additional course ideas or new directions for the school to pursue.

"You need to offer a major in this field."

"You know there's a real need in the marketplace for this service."

"If you had this event, I know there would be a great response."

Employees, customers and church members will have their own agendas for us, making focus the biggest challenge we face at every level of leadership. While their ideas may be worthy of consideration, they can distract us from our mission. Each morning we come to the office with a plan, but if we're not careful, our plans get shifted by the plans of others. Our calendars will get filled. We should be the ones to fill them.

We've all had days when we didn't feel like we accomplished anything. We feel like a Ferrari driving through a school zone; we can't give it our full power. We've given ten percent to this project and twelve percent to that project, but we haven't pushed the gas pedal all the way down on any one project. How can we ever accomplish anything this way?

Satan may never tempt us to rob a bank, sniff cocaine or cheat on our spouses. If he can keep us from accomplishing anything, he doesn't have to. Rather than knock us out of our jobs through sin, he can keep us in our jobs doing nothing. We can stay and be ineffectual, and he wins. What he can't pollute, he will dilute.

As our organizations grow, there will always be more to distract us. If we look around at our growing organizations and see that the people are confused, before blaming them we need to stop and ask, "How focused am I?" When we get out of focus, our people are unsure how to respond and unable to move forward.

WARNING SIGNS

Signs of being distracted include the following:

1) *Getting Marginalized.* Our input and influence are reduced or limited to only a few areas. Decisions are made without our input or we attend meetings to vote on an issue, and it doesn't matter because the votes needed have already been decided.

2) *Being Diverted.* Nonessential things occupy our time and thoughts, or resources are used for things that aren't necessary.

3) *Getting Attacked.* Resistance and overt attacks remove our focus from the main issues. As I said earlier, it may not be a headlining sin that Satan uses to attack us; it might be a whole lot of small distractions.

4) *Getting Seduced.* Pleasing our allies becomes more important than staying on a difficult course.

We know that keeping focus is hard. You may even find it hard to continue reading because of all the distractions you're facing right now. But if you stop reading every time your phone rings, an email comes in or a social media notification pops up, you'll never get to the solutions you are hoping to find. Keeping focus is difficult even when you know what it is.

THE MEANING OF FOCUS

Focus means putting the important things first and leaving everything else for second. If we can cut out the unimportant and unify behind the vision, we'll always have focus. Of course, the most important thing is sticking with it.

But to have focus in our churches and organizations, not only do we have to be focused, but so does everyone who works with us. We have to teach them to be focused as soon as we hire or recruit them.

Most leaders can do eight things at once and do them all well. But sometimes they mistakenly have the same expectations for the people who work for them. As leaders, they're used to multitasking and are proud of it, so they inadvertently encourage it in the people who work for them. They even say things like, "Around here, everybody wears five hats."

While it is true that there are times in an organization's history and growth when everyone needs to step up and wear as many as fifteen hats, as the organization grows we've got to bring in people who are skilled in specific areas, and we need to empower them to pursue those tasks, making sure that other roles are not dumped in their laps, just because they are competent in the ones we hired them for.

Often leaders hire someone and say, "Thirty percent of the time you will be doing this, and seventy percent of the time you will be doing that." It sounds good and may even look good on paper, but the main thing often becomes the thing that is most neglected. Ultimately, it won't be the employee's fault; it will be the fault of the leader who didn't keep her focused. As leaders, we must help those around us to understand and stick to their focus.

And we must stick to ours. Sometimes we may be tempted to help our people do their jobs, rather than lead them. We'll know we're gravitating toward doing the work, rather than leading, when we make these types of statements:

"Here, I can do that for you."

"I'll help you finish that; I've done one like it before."

"Let's sit down and go over all the things you need for the project."

"Yeah, we did that program at my last church. Let me get some stuff out of my files for you."

If everyone in the organization, including the leader, wears only one hat, then we can ask for and get higher levels of accountability and performance. Our focus should be on leading people to the right hat and helping them keep it on their heads.

THE FLOW OF FOCUS

How do we find our focus? Maybe we think that grabbing a legal pad and making a list of the things we need to do can determine our focus. We take the list of eighteen or 118 jobs and try to combine items to make big rocks out of all of our little rocks. Then we prioritize those rocks and pick one rock as our focus for the day. We think that making a list will bring about focus. But the to-do list only shows us *what* we're focusing on. *What* we focus on should always flow from *who* we are.

The starting place for finding focus should always be questions like: *Who am I? If I were to die today, what would I most regret leaving unfinished?*

Once we define *who* we are, then we can do the *what* because the what has to flow out of our *who*. This is true for our entire organizations because the organization is a reflection of the leader's vision, or the leader's *who*. How we accomplish our visions is *what* we do. Our organizations can't do the *what* until they understand the *who*.

A church's programs should be the result of the leader's vision for the church. If a program doesn't fit the vision, the church shouldn't be doing it. It doesn't mean it's a bad program; it only means that it isn't for the church at this time.

It is important to find our focus, but we also need to know that, at different times in our lives, our focus will change. As we get older, there's something within us that says, "I want to give more time to fewer things." Our focus will narrow even further.

FOCUS IS COMMUNICABLE

Once we know what our focus is, we need to communicate it throughout our organizations. The actual process of succinctly communicating vision can actually help us sharpen our focus. We need to be able to communicate it in small sound bites. If we can't condense the vision to something that fits on a T-shirt, are we really that focused? Or could we further refine the focus? Second, our people are more likely to work toward our vision if they are clear on what it is.

Many people go to work to do a job. They learn specific things like how to use software or how to build a truck. But when we take time to teach people *why* they are doing *what* they are doing, we help them to have a deeper understanding of their focus. Suddenly, they aren't only building trucks; they're creating reliable transportation for people who deliver food to families via the supermarket. No longer are they entering names into a software database. Instead, they are making sure that visitors to the church will be promptly ministered to. By sharing who we are and how what they do relates to our vision, we teach them that who they are is also important.

Getting people to think at this level will increase the dialogue about focus within the organization. If we invite honest and open conversations, we may find that the people around us start asking difficult and probing questions. At first this may make us uncomfortable, but we shouldn't feel threatened. Questions are signs that they are thinking at an organizational level. This kind of dialogue can help our people to make better decisions and use their time and resources more wisely.

Our focus is our light. Diffused, it can still brighten a room. But when concentrated, focused into a laser beam, there is not a more powerful leadership tool.

CHAPTER 5

COMMUNICATION

*The leader has to be practical and a realist, yet must talk
the language of the visionary and the idealist.*
—Eric Hoffer, American philosopher

Thinkers come in two kinds: concrete or abstract. Their communication style follows their preferred way of thinking. Leaders are generally abstract thinkers. They talk in vague platitudes. They are great visionaries. But followers or doers are generally concrete thinkers. When they talk, they use specific, concrete terms. The difference in the communication styles between leaders and followers can lead to confusion.

Now as leaders, this is where we often mess up. We don't consider how our abstract messages will be received by the concrete thinkers in the organizations we lead. We just throw it out without any regard to how they will hear it. For example, a pastor will tell his congregation, "Today I am going to cast a vision, and then next Sunday I am going to come back and tell you how we're going to fulfill that vision and give you the details of our strategy."

This is a bad idea.

When concrete thinkers don't have enough information, they take what they hear and fill in the details. Then they pour mental concrete, the quick-set kind, on top of it. The following Sunday, we will have to blast their concrete thinking out of the water in order to lay the foundation we want laid. Essentially, we come back to them and ask them to change their minds.

Leaders who are abstract thinkers need to become concrete communicators. We need to provide details when we cast the vision. This allows us to pour our own concrete. We get to quickly set the vision the way we want it set.

When the president of the company says that there will be a major reorganization without providing any details of what that reorganization looks like, some of the best employees will be at their desks looking for new jobs because they think it means they're being fired.

As leaders we can be both concrete and abstract; but our followers or employees may only think concretely. We can broadcast in both AM and FM, but they can only hear AM. We have to make sure we broadcast the vision in a way the receiver can hear it. To do this, we need to give our people the abstract and the concrete at the same time.

BAD COMMUNICATION HABITS

Communicating only when we need something. We can't be the kind of leaders who only speak to our teams when we need something. No employee wants to feel like he or she is only there to serve the boss. As leaders, we need to be conscious of how we treat the people around us.

Not following up. The best-laid plans will never do more than gather dust unless we actually do something to implement them. Poor implementation and lack of execution are often made worse because of our sloppy communication patterns. To see more work completed we need to hold people accountable. We can do this by ending our meetings, emails and conversations with a few key questions:

- What is the next step?

- When will it be completed?

- By whom?

A little bit of follow-through each time we communicate will result in a whole lot of execution.

Not returning phone calls or emails. Many people lie on their answering machines. "Please leave a message, and I will get back with you." Instead, it should say, "Just leave a message, and if I feel like it, I will call you back. If I don't call you back, it means I didn't want to talk to you; so just chill."

Not only is it common courtesy to respond to someone, not responding allows others to pour the concrete. If they can't get an answer from me, they will get an answer somewhere else, and it may not be the answer I want them to have. Here's what I do when I don't have time to give them a full answer. Perhaps I get an e-mail with eighteen questions I can't answer, I respond as soon as I open it and say, "I will read it and respond to you in a few days."

Even though I can't answer all of their questions immediately, they aren't left to wonder whether or not I got the e-mail. They receive a reply and know that I am on top of it. We all know how frustrating it is to send something and never hear back. We can't follow through with people if we don't talk to them in the first place.

Lack of basic courtesy. I hope I don't even have to say this, but when communicating with people, use basic courtesy. Say please and thank you. Sometimes when people work in close proximity, they forget the small niceties:

"Will you please do this?"

"Thank you for the report."

"You're welcome."

"My pleasure."

"Anytime."

Think how the atmosphere around the office could change if everybody used basic courtesy.

Focusing on the negative. Some people have a gift for grabbing the negativity in any situation and holding on. The most important thing a leader does for his people is to push back their horizons and put blue-sky thinking into their lives. We need to pull the positive out and add value to it rather than focusing on what was going wrong. Help put some BS (blue sky) into their thinking!

Not Listening. When people talk about communication, they usually talk about sending the message; they rarely talk about listening to it. But for any message to be effective, someone must receive it. If we're not listening to the people around us, we're not good communicators. Hearing what someone else says not only helps us to understand what he says, but it helps us to know how to respond to him as well. Listening is an art we can cultivate. Active listening includes observing body language and making eye contact with the person we are with. It is how we sit when we deliver a message and how we respond to questions.

LISTENING AND ANSWERING

Now what does *listening* have to do with answering questions? By really listening, we can hear the question the person is asking. Sometimes people don't ask the question they really want answered. For example, if a mother of a young child says, "Is the planning meeting *really* at 5:00 today?" she may be wanting more than a confirmation of the time and place. She may be thinking, *How late is that meeting going to go because I have to pick up my child at the babysitter's?*

If we answer her question with a "yes," we won't have really answered her question. She will continue to be frustrated that she can't be in two places at one time.

Instead, if we observe her body language and listen to the way she phrases the question, we can respond differently, "Something seems to be bothering you." Then she can tell us that she has to pick up her child, that the presentation won't be ready in time, or that she was hoping to get approval on the plans before noon. A "yes," while technically correct, may cause us to miss information that she wouldn't volunteer without a little coaxing. We wouldn't even know to prompt her for more information unless we heard what she was trying to say without words. Remember the first question presented is never the real question. The question behind the question is the real question.

Listening is more important than speaking. Close observation and thoughtful responses can help people know that we hear what they are really trying to say. By paying attention to others when we communicate, we'll always be able to give the right answer, even when we don't have one.

What do we typically do when we come across a discussion? Many of us jump right to the answer giving. We miss some of the best opportunities to communicate because everywhere we go, we talk. We never go simply to listen. When there are three or four people in the hallway, we never stand there and become part of the group; we want to be the one who gives the answers.

As leaders, we need to do more listening. We need to resist being the one who knows it all. By listening to others, we learn how to communicate more effectively with both abstract and concrete communicators. We receive better information from those around us, and then we gain a greater understanding of the situation. If our conversations turn to conflict, they will occupy too much of our thinking. Here are some actions I learned to do when communicating:

Try to empathetically understand her concern.

- Realistically determine if she is a won't or a can't. A won't is about attitude; a can't is about ability. Both can be helped, but in different ways.

- Don't attach spiritual issues to a lack of response.

- Make sure I am broadcasting on her frequency.

Remember it is my responsibility as a leader to communicate effectively. The most important conversations are always going to be the ones we have with ourselves. The conversations in my head regarding people with whom communication doesn't come easy were filled with anger, doubt and frustration. Stopping to listen to what I was telling myself, as well as taking a communication time-out to reassess the situation, showed me that I needed to be the first to change.

Learning to listen to others and to our own self-talk will help us respond appropriately, even to the ones who frustrate us.

CHAPTER 6
DECISION-MAKING

When you're 100% certain, you're too late.
—Charles W. Robinson

A leader, by definition, makes decisions—decisions that affect the future of organizations and the people that comprise them. Either we are situational decision makers or principled decision makers, and we communicate which of these we are by the decisions we make. Decision-making is predictable when done by a principled leader. What I mean by this is that employees of a principled leader feel secure because decisions are consistent, and the leader considers long-term consequences before making them.

In contrast, situational leaders rarely think about future consequences. They are mostly interested in avoiding conflict right now. Their decisions are inconsistent. People who work for situational leaders are rarely sure how the decision will be made. Employees may try to control the information the leader receives in an effort to influence his or her decision in a direction that is favorable to them. Working for a situational leader can be very difficult because the employee is always trying to second guess what the leader's response will be, for it is rarely the same twice.

It is important for us to understand how we make decisions because our decisions tell other people who we are.

A DECISION-MAKING MODEL

Decision-making is an art and a science. Sadly, most of us were never taught how to make good decisions, so we make them based on the situation. But we can learn to make better decisions if we analyze the steps we use.

Each time we make a decision, we follow several steps. Most of these happen unconsciously. The most common steps include gathering data, sorting out the information that is relevant to the decision, combining it with our knowledge and then ultimately making a decision. Here's a closer look at these steps, but let's use a rather mundane example that anyone can relate to.

Pat lives in North Georgia and needs to travel to South Atlanta for Grandma's birthday party. Doesn't seem like much of a decision, does it? Pat loves her cooking, and nothing is better than spending Sunday dinner at Grandma's house since she always makes a feast. But to get to her house while the mashed potatoes are still hot, Pat has to make many decisions. Here's a demonstration of one: How will he get to Grandmother's house?

Step One: Collect Data.

During this step, we collect all of the data that we need or could possibly need. For Pat, that data might include the answers to these questions:

- What time does dinner start?

- How early does he need to get there to get a seat at the adult table?

- What time does the Sunday worship service start and end at his church?

- Does he need to go home first, or can he leave directly after church?

- Will he be attending Sunday School that day?

- What subject will the pastor preach on?

- How long does it take to get to Grandma's?

- Will he be hungry when he gets there?

- Will he take I-75 or Highway 400?

- Which is the fastest route? Safest route?

Step Two: Select Relevant Information.

At this point, Pat has to select which pieces of data are relevant to his decision. Whether or not he will be hungry and the topic of the pastor's sermon on Sunday won't affect his travel plans, so he can safely eliminate those pieces. By comparing and connecting the other bits of data, he can get information that is actually useful. Consider some pieces that will be meaningful for the decision he is about to make:

He plans to attend the worship service at his church. It ends at 11:00.

Grandma wants him at her place by 1:00.

There are several ways to get there. If he takes Interstate 75, it will take approximately an hour and a half.

Currently there is construction on I-75, and the traffic could delay him up to forty-five minutes.

If he takes State Highway 400, it will take an hour and forty-five minutes, but there isn't any construction.

Step Three: Combine with Preexisting Knowledge.

Now that Pat has the relevant information, he can combine it with preexisting knowledge, such as the fact that if he is late for dinner not only will Grandma be mad, but Cousin Arthur will finish off the banana cream pie.

Step Four: Make the Decision.

At this point, Pat decides he will take Highway 400 because, while it may not get him there earlier, it will ensure that he is at Grandma's house on time. And the consequences of being late (and missing Grandma's banana cream pie) are too great. Decision made.

Obviously, in this example Pat is probably making this decision intuitively, but that intuitive process follows the same pattern as a more significant decision. We follow these same steps each time we make a decision; however, with most decisions, we do it so fast that we aren't conscious of it. This model tries to diagram that unconscious process, whether our choices involve driving directions, leadership or even dating decisions. Regardless of the context, these same four steps are involved.

Understanding how we make decisions can help us get better at solving problems because we can test our assumptions at each step in the process. For example, if the data that we used to make a decision was wrong, the decision won't be a good one. If we incorrectly categorized or utilized information that wasn't relevant, that step will influence our decisions. If our preexisting knowledge is wrong, then combining it with excellent data will still lead to a poor choice.

The ability to articulate each of the steps in our thinking process can help us to make better decisions. It can also lead to better relationships with the people we work with.

AN OPPORTUNITY TO COMMUNICATE

As leaders, we are not the only ones making decisions, and we often deal with the consequences of others' decision-making. When those around us make bad decisions, don't just come down hard on them; use this time as an opportunity to talk with them. Ask them how they made the decision. What process did they go through? Using the decision-making model from above, ask them what data they started with. How did they decide which pieces of information were relevant to their decision? What existing knowledge did they combine with the data to make their decision?

Asking these kinds of questions will help us understand more about how they approach their own decision-making. More importantly, it will become an opportunity for us to teach them regarding how we would like them to make decisions in the future.

We can also explain why we did what we did, using this as an opportunity to refocus them on the vision, teach them better decision-making skills and learn how their decision-making patterns differ from our own. In any organization, the better we understand our own decision-making blind spots and the blind spots of those who work with us, the better we can conquer them.

FOUR QUESTIONS

When presented with a complicated decision that could change the organization, we need to ask four questions, and it is important that we ask them *in this order:*

1) *Is it in line with our vision, mission, and core values?* No matter how great an idea or opportunity, if it isn't in line with the vision, we must say no to it.

2) *Do we have the organizational and human capacity to do this?* Do we have the heart for this? Maybe the program is so large that it would tax the entire team. Maybe we don't have the right people on the team to make this happen. Or maybe we don't want to do it at this time.

3) *How will God be glorified?* Most leaders will ask, "Will God be glorified?" and the answer is usually yes. Instead, ask, "How?" Answering this question will help us understand the true impact this decision will have on God's kingdom. Those in the secular marketplace can ask the same question with a slight twist: "How will this decision serve the community or my organization?"

4) *How much will it cost?* Understand this question, and then consider it carefully. It is not, "Can we afford it?" Most organizations don't have money sitting around waiting to be used. The answer is usually no. But the answer to "How much will it cost?" is different. The cost includes not only dollars, but people, resources and the time and energy pulled from other projects and programs.

There's a reason the question of cost is last. A program that won't make it past the question "Can we afford it?" might get a different response after asking these four questions. If the vision is big enough, if the people have a heart for doing it, if God will be glorified in a mighty way, then the money will come.

Answering these specific questions, *in this order,* helps us understand the true opportunity before us. We will be making a principled decision based on a larger organizational context, not on a situation, such as the amount of cash in the checkbook.

PRACTICAL DECISION-MAKING

The information above gives us a foundation for making good decisions, but there are a few practical tips that will help us as well.

Be able to explain why. We need to be able to articulate why we made the decision we did. This isn't so we can defend ourselves when we make a bad decision; it is so we can learn from all of our decisions. If we don't know why we did it in the first place, we will never get better at making decisions. Understanding how we make decisions will help us to make even better decisions in the future.

Be brave. Sometimes when we make decisions, we want to stay in our comfort zone and not go outside of it for additional data. This is a bad idea. Whenever possible we should seek information from those people or places that have it, even if it makes us uncomfortable. For example, ask:

- "Who on my team will show me the things I most need to see?"

- "Who will tell me things that are hard to hear?"

- "Who is the best source for the information needed to make this decision?"

Be decisive. We won't always have all the information we need to make a decision. Sometimes the best thing we can do is make a decision without having all of the information. How do we know which decisions should wait and which we should move on? Put time into the decisions with the biggest payoff. Allow others to make those to which we can add little, even if we like making them.

Be willing to smash icons. We can't let turf wars, misuse of power or phony motivation schemes affect our judgment. Resist the idea that loyalty is a one-way street. Junk short-term strategies that prevent long-term successes.

We make many decisions each day. Some of them are important, some of them are not. But the more we can pay attention to the process we use in making decisions, the better decisions we will make. As we climb the rungs of the leadership ladder, the number of decisions we will make exponentially grows, and the impact of those decisions broadens.

CHAPTER 7
CHANGE & TRANSITION

Life is pleasant. Death is peaceful. It's the transition that's troublesome.
—Isaac Asimov, novelist and scholar

Change is the result of a decision. It is an external event. Transition, on the other hand, is the emotional, relational, financial and psychological processing of change. Transitions are internal.

Understanding the difference between change and transition can help leaders plan appropriately. It is rare that change itself causes problems; typically, the culprit is a lack of transitional planning. Leaders are responsible for foreseeing and creating a strategy for transition in their organizations. But often, we spend so much time on change, we never strategically think through the transitional issues.

To be a good CEO or pastor, it isn't enough to only think through what we're going to do. We must also take time to write down all of the contingencies and create a written transitional plan. What situation results from this change? Personnel issues that need thought include:

- Which people does the change affect?

- Of those people, who are the ones who care?

- Who cares deeply?

- Of those who care deeply, who will be positive about this change and who will not?

This is the main question: How do I position the people I lead for success? After thinking through these questions, the leader must create a written plan and then make strategic decisions based on the plan. For example, consider:

- How will I approach each person?

- How will I communicate the details to him or her?

- What information will that person need to understand this change?

HOW TO TRANSITION

William Bridges is a noted expert on change and transition. In his book, *Managing Transitions: Making the Most of Change,* he explains that the reason change agents fail is because they focus on the solution instead of the problem. He believes that ninety percent of a leader's efforts should be spent on selling the problem and helping people understand what is *not* working. He rightly claims that people don't perceive the need for a solution if they don't have a problem.

Let's say I have an administrative assistant who is not working out. She comes in late, has a bad attitude and is incompetent in her job. Firing her would solve that problem, but before I can fire her, I need to consider how this action would affect her coworkers. Currently she gets a lot of sympathy from them. They enable her behavior and encourage me to do the same by saying things like, "Don't you realize she's pregnant and recently had to change apartments?"

This is also where lawsuits can become transitional issues. Firing a pregnant woman without cause could bring legal trouble for me and the company. I must be sure the problem is understood. Of course, I am aware that she is failing to be a good assistant, but I have to help others in the office understand that her inability to do her job is a problem for all of us. If I don't, they will be the first to undermine me by saying to the new assistant, "Did you know that he fired the pregnant woman who was here before you?"

Part of the transition must be helping people understand the problem so they can more quickly agree on a solution.

Before I resigned from the college, I personally traveled all over the country to meet with board members and tell them what I was going to do and why. I even developed a possible successor.

There are no smooth transitions, because smooth means everything goes exactly as planned. There are only good transitions or poorly executed ones. Of course, I wanted a seamless changeover, but I knew better. We always face the IBs—the inevitable bumps. Our best-laid plans usually don't work out.

In making that change, I had a transition plan. I knew who I was going to talk to, when I was going to talk to them, and what I was going to say. I can vouch from my personal experience that the time spent thinking and planning the transition made what could have been a negative occurrence a time of positive growth for me and the college.

CHANGE WITHOUT TRANSITION

A successful transition isn't the responsibility of the people undergoing the change. The responsibility for a successful transition belongs to the leader making the change. In one of my seminars, a young woman named Regina said she was moved from a small role in the children's department to a larger responsibility as Christian education minister. Regina did everything she could to prepare her people for a change. She found and trained her successor and helped transition her old team to their new leader.

But no one did the same for Regina. The pastor failed to make an announcement to the church that Regina was given this new responsibility. Further complicating matters, the former Christian education minister didn't realize that he was now out of a job and continued to function as if nothing had changed. This is a great example of a change without a transition. Regina had made the change, but without her pastor helping with the transition, she was now impotent in her new responsibility.

Some might wonder why a pastor would do that. I think I know. Regina is his daughter, and he was worried about how people would react to her taking on such an important role. He felt that she was the best person for the job, and she felt that she was ready. But without handling the transition properly, no one else at the church had that same confidence. Now he was trying to sort through the mess. He has both personal issues (after all, she's his daughter) and professional issues (his vision for this position in the church). In addition, when I first heard about the situation, Regina had been in her job for three months!

My recommendation to Regina was that her father go before the people and say, "My daughter, Regina, is going to provide great leadership to the Christian education ministry department at our church. Actually, she should have been functioning in this position for the last three months, but I have been remiss in not making that announcement. I'm correcting that today. Come on up here, Regina, and tell them about your vision. What's God going to do with you?"

He will need to support her vision and have the people pray for her in her new role, sort of as a mini-inauguration. But he has to say something like, "I was remiss in not doing this before," so the people will know why he is doing this now and not then.

Assimilating new people into leadership roles is the hardest change issue we face. However, if we as leaders are aware of the differences between transitions and changes, if we properly prepare and execute a transitional plan, and if we take responsibility for the changes we bring on our people, the results will be worth the effort.

CHAPTER 8
CONFLICT

Everybody in America is soft, and hates conflict. The cure for this, both in politics and social life, is the same—hardihood.
—John Jay Chapman, author

There is no such thing as a conflict-free zone. The only way to eliminate conflict is not to do anything. As long as there is movement or activity, engagement or involvement, there will always be conflict. Conflict management is an unavoidable rung on the leadership ladder. When a leader tells me that he has a peaceful organization and that everybody gets along with everybody, I think, *Either you're out of touch or you're not doing anything.*

Sometimes we are so afraid of conflict that we strive for peace and consensus when a little conflict might actually help the cause. A lack of conflict doesn't signal progress, but it might signal inactivity. Conflict is something that will always be. It is neither good nor bad, it simply is.

THE BENEFITS OF CONFLICT

Conflict serves a purpose. When there is conflict, we explore the issues surrounding that conflict more fully. The associated tension causes us to look deeper into a decision to make sure that we have all the information we need and aren't overlooking anything. Conflict becomes the motivation to make sure we examine the situation in detail. No one wants to be on the wrong side of an issue he or she didn't fully investigate. When conflict is involved, people are often more committed to the final decision because they are confident that the issues have been examined from all sides and the best solution has been reached.

For conflict to be used positively it must involve dialogue with opposing parties *before* the decision is made. The actual process of making the decision becomes more important than the decision itself. Even people with contrary views will respond positively, or at least "agree to disagree," if they feel like their side was heard and understood by those making the decision.

THE DARK SIDE OF CONFLICT

But conflict can have a dark side as well. Consider a leader who faces unnecessary conflict over every decision she tries to make. It is like an electric fence used to keep a dog in the yard. The dog can't see it, but he knows not to cross the edge of the property line because he will get a mild shock. After attempting it several times, the dog soon learns it's better to avoid the borders altogether. When this happens to a leader, she is tempted to walk away from issues she needs to address because she fears the conflict. As a result, conflict can limit the scope of our leadership and make leaders reluctant to lead.

Likewise, personal conflict can affect our jobs. If I have a fight with my wife on the way to church on Sunday morning, by the time I get to the pulpit and begin to preach, she is all I can think about. I see her scowling at me from the front row, and I know she's thinking, *If only the people knew what I know. He should be the first one in line for the altar call!* It is hard to do a job well when distracted, and conflict in one area can leak into others. If we have conflict at work, it is hard not to bring that home to the family.

BLOOD ON THE FLOOR

The desire to avoid tough issues and distractions caused by conflict can skew our normally good judgment. Instead of facing conflict, we run from it. When we suppress our best instincts in an attempt to keep peace, we're not being true to our callings.

We've all heard this old adage: "You can't please everybody." What I wish someone had told me was, "Sam, there will be blood on the floor. It may be yours, or it may be theirs, but to get where you're going, you may have to pay for it in blood." Of course, even if I had heard it, I probably wasn't in a place to understand it until I had been through it. But now I've learned; there is a price to be paid. Please understand, we can minimize the blood, but the blood will still be there.

Of course, I am not talking about literal blood on the floor; I am talking about the painful feelings aroused when we work through conflict. I am also talking about the sacrifices made in the process. When my father disciplined me, he never drew real blood. But the shame of my actions often made me feel as if my blood had been spilled.

Some people like me; some people don't. We are all born with a need to be liked and approved, but sometimes in an effort to be accepted, we avoid necessary conflict. While I am not suggesting that we be conflict-lovers, we do need to find a way to come to terms with conflict, to be able to say, "I can't please everybody, and conflict is going to happen. It doesn't matter who I am or where I am at, sometimes there is just going to be blood on the floor."

HEALTHY CONFLICT

If I cut my finger, it's going to scab over and heal. Depending on the size and location of the cut, it might leave a scar. But since I am healthy, it will eventually heal. If I were unhealthy, or if I were a hemophiliac, the bleeding would be much harder to stop. I might get an infection or even bleed to death.

We need to view conflict in terms of our overall health. There is no such thing as a good marriage or a bad marriage, a good church or a bad church. There are only healthy marriages and unhealthy marriages, healthy churches and unhealthy churches.

The biggest factor in any conflict is the condition of the leader's health. We must be healthy when dealing with conflict.

We need to ask:

- ■ "Is this interaction healthy?"

- ■ "Is the way she's looking at me healthy?"

- ■ "The way I'm looking back, is that healthy?"

- ■ "What I'm just thinking, is that healthy?"

We shouldn't try to end conflict in agreement or disagreement; we should try to end it healthily. If the ultimate goal is agreement, the stakes are high, and one side will always be the loser. Instead, at the end of any difficult dialogue, we should always ask, "Are we still healthy?" because healthy relationships allow for transparency and open communication. The healthier the relationship, the more the transparency.

WHAT VS. WHO

Just because someone disagrees with me doesn't mean he is against me. My wife disagrees with me all the time. She isn't against me; she just disagrees. Anytime someone moves from the what to the who, it gets personal and people get defensive. Instead of getting solved, the problem escalates. We need to first deal with the *what* before we can deal with the *who*.

Always deal with the situation, and stay there for as long as possible before dealing with the person responsible. However, sometimes the who is the problem. If Mary has a problem with Dewayne, and Mary has a problem with Susan, and Mary has a problem with Gaye, the problem isn't Dewayne, Susan and Gaye; the problem is Mary. John Maxwell calls people like Mary "conflict carriers."

It doesn't matter where they go; conflict carriers create problems. Perhaps Mary is an employee who routinely disrupts the entire staff. I can go to Mary one-on-one and say, "This is totally unacceptable behavior." Then I can explain what I expect from her and tell her that if it isn't possible for her to live up to those expectations, I will have to let her go.

But before I have that conversation, I need to have a conversation in which I help her understand what she is doing, so she has an opportunity to correct her disruptive behavior. I need to try the redemptive pathway first.

However, the suggestion comes with a warning. People like Mary can hijack a conversation because they want to talk specific issues while we want to talk about patterns of behavior. If I begin the conversation by saying, "Yesterday at the office . . . ," immediately she will get defensive and try to give me reasons for what happened yesterday. If I say, "There was a problem between you and Allen," immediately she's going to talk about Allen.

I need to control the conversation and frame it around the larger pattern. I need to say to her, "I've noticed conflict simmering at different times and in different ways." Then I follow with, "I really don't want to talk about any specific instance, but there seems to be a pattern here. Can you help me understand what might be going on?"

I must be especially careful with the tone of my voice and my facial expressions. The conversation needs to take place in an informal setting. Conflict carriers put their radar up if we put them into formal situations. Authority figures cause problems for conflict carriers, so never have this conversation from the other side of a desk. Make it low key, informal, friendly and warm. Don't go in with any agenda except to understand where the person is.

Always preface the conversation by saying, "I have noticed a pattern," and describing the pattern. Plug the holes that she will use to escape by saying, "Listen, Mary, I don't want to talk about anything specific. That's not going to help us right now. But you can help me understand what might be going on." Then patiently wait to see where she takes the conversation, gently nudging her back to the pattern when she runs for the details.

Never say to a conflict carrier, "People have told me. . . ." If I say that, she will only become defensive and argumentative. I have to take ownership and say, "I have noticed. . . ." and then ask if she can help me understand.

She'll try another tactic: "Well, Arthur talked to you about this."

Don't go there. Keep focused. "Just help me understand; there's a pattern over here." She is most comfortable with specifics because she has information; the patterns are harder for her to defend.

If I can do this action successfully, I will have a new opportunity to get through to Mary. If I make the mistake of focusing on a specific, the conversation is over. I have to be assertive in setting up the parameters of the conversation.

Some people will not have the spiritual maturity to receive that advice, but I still believe we should try. As leaders, we need to look at ourselves in the mirror and know that we did everything we could. We want to go the second mile, and we can do that only if we're healthy. Our health comes from being secure in our setting, confident that where God has placed us is where we are supposed to be. From this position, we can consistently navigate conflict and lead our organizations.

CHAPTER 9

ALIGNMENT

Every company has two organizational structures: The formal one is written on the charts; the other is the everyday relationship of the men and women in the organization.
—Harold S. Geneen, former chairman, ITT

Many leaders have faced the circumstance in which they joined a church or company with a vision for one thing, but over time the vision shifted to something else. At first the leader goes along because it's not a big deal. Ministry leaders and board members will offer ideas, suggestions, and plans that sound great, but are not in alignment with the original vision. The leader doesn't want to discourage the creativity of those people, so he smiles and goes along. *It can't hurt anything, can it?* he wonders. *It's all for God's good, right?*

But eventually a morning comes when the leader wakes up and realizes that the organization's vision is different from his own. In this situation, many leaders say, "I can adjust my vision," and they try following the direction set by the organization. It's easier to adjust their own sense of God's calling and vision than to expend all the energy it would require to bring the entire leadership team, plans and programs back into alignment with the original vision.

This will never work.

The leader cannot catch up to a parade that has started without her. Even if she makes it to the front in time, how can she lead when she doesn't know where the members are going? The leader has subordinated *her* God-given vision to a group of people who are journeying elsewhere. It might be that their destination and vision are as worthy as hers, but the point is this: It isn't hers. It isn't what God gave *her* to do.

An organization must be in line with the leader's vision and core values. If they aren't, how can he lead it? A CEO with principles can't lead a subordinate who doesn't believe in rules. A pastor can't focus if his people aren't supporting the vision he is focused on. Organizational alignment is necessary if a church or organization wants to be functional.

WHAT IS ORGANIZATIONAL ALIGNMENT?

When a leader's vision and values are aligned with the organization's goals, the alignment will be reflected in everything they do.

For example, a local Atlanta church states that one of its core values is missions. This core value is demonstrated in everything the members do. The budget shows a large percentage of their income going to missions projects. The missions department has more people than any other department. The calendar reveals that much of the scheduling is for missions-related activities. Likewise, if both children's ministry and the missions department both wanted to meet with the pastor and he had time for only one meeting, he would choose the missions department. This focus demonstrates organizational alignment.

Another example is a business that boasts their focus is on customer service. To check, I would look at their personnel files to see how many people actually worked with customers. I would review their training and see what they are paid. I would look at all the ways customers contact the business and then see who handles those contacts and in what order of priority. I would also look to see how they treat their employees because if morale is high and conflict is low, they can serve the customer better. Customer service is either a priority or it isn't. If it is, everything about the corporation should demonstrate it.

Organizational alignment begins with our focus. It flows from our vision, mission and core values; and it permeates every area of our organization. If it doesn't, we don't have alignment.

ALIGNMENT AND STRATEGIC PLANNING

Alignment is reflected in how an organization approaches strategic planning, the process by which the vision is translated into an actionable plan which addresses personnel, resources, goals, a timeline and so on.

Strategic planning enables a team and every department in an organization to work together for a common goal. It's the hallmark of alignment, and it's essential to healthy organizational culture.

Strategic planning is an acquired skill. When a team learns the principles of strategic planning and gains some experience, it becomes second nature for them to value the alignment of vision, people, and resources. A healthy, powerful culture moves a team and an organization toward the ultimate objectives God has given them.

The strategic planning process involves a series of meetings in which the following questions are asked *and* answered:

- What is our vision?

- Why are we doing this? How does it relate to our core values?

- Who is responsible? What will they do?

- How do we plan to do this? (Be specific.)

- When will this be done? What are the due dates for specific tasks, and who will accomplish them?

- How much will this cost? Do we have the capacity (people, facilities, finances, etc.) to undertake this right now?

- To whom are we accountable for this?

- How will we measure success?

Once the staff is familiar with strategic planning details, the questions and answers will fly from different parts of the room until the terms of a concrete plan are agreed on. That's the beauty of teaching strategic planning to the staff. Soon they will be doing it without realizing they are doing it.

Remember, this isn't a process to help the team make decisions. I covered decision-making questions in an earlier chapter. Strategic planning is the process of making sure the decisions we've already made will be strategically implemented. Taking time to put meat on the bones of an idea will help to ensure that something actually gets done. When things start to change, transitions will be easier, conflict will be reduced and organizational alignment will increase.

This process also helps to ensure that there is alignment between the people and the structure of an organization. Not only do we have to make sure that our vision and the organization are in alignment, we also need to make sure that we align people within the organizational structure, so they can create results.

PEOPLE OVER STRUCTURE

When things aren't working, leaders often prefer to change the formal structure of an organization because it is the easiest area to tackle. Moving boxes around on an organizational chart, reassigning who reports to whom, and handing out new titles doesn't require much management ability. It is a clean process. It is logical.

In most organizations, reorganizing the structure won't make people work better or harder. It is like the man who needs to clean out his garage but decides to organize his bedroom closet because it is easier.

It may be easier, but the results won't be a cleaner garage. What's really important isn't the formal details of the job—it's the people in the job.

To change things in an organization, adjustments must be made to the informal connections, not the formal structure. These informal processes and behaviors can be troublesome, but when handled properly, the results are worth the effort.

Larry Bossidy, chairman and CEO of Honeywell, said, "People have told me I spend too much time on people, but I know that if I get the best people, I am going to walk away with the prize. In this day and age, organizations that don't have the best people don't win." People must take priority over structure.

Leaders prefer to change the formal structure because it is easier than changing people. Reorganizing the structure won't bring people into alignment. To be effective, changes must be made to the informal connections, not the formal structure.

It's important to understand that organizational alignment is not about the specific programs or the projects that our organizations initiate. Nor is it about keeping people in line. Rather, it is keeping alignment between people, vision and structure. Alignment is getting all the parts to work as one body. For good.

CHAPTER 10
MONEY

Money is a terrible master but an excellent servant.
—P. T. Barnum

When I first became a college president, I didn't even know what an audit looked like. I had never seen one before. I didn't understand what restricted or unrestricted funds were, I had no idea what depreciation was, and the various categories of numbers made no sense at all to me. The first time I was presented with an audit, it was page after page of nothing but numbers. At the bottom of the page, in tiny print, were a lot of disclaimers. They were written in some sort of accountant-speak.

Just because you have ascended several rungs of the leadership ladder does not automatically mean that you have an equivalent knowledge of the financial and legal details of your organization. In fact, entrepreneurial leaders often have unique gaps in knowledge due to the unconventional paths they have taken to reach their positions of responsibility.

Likewise, pastors are overwhelmed, and they should be. They may not have received the training they needed to succeed at their jobs because, until recently, seminaries didn't offer courses in business management. Due to recent corporate accounting scandals, even businesses are now facing more financial and legal scrutiny than ever before.

Despite our lack of training in these areas, we still are required to conform to the laws and regulations of governing bodies: Occupational Safety and Health Administration (OSHA), generally accepted accounting procedures (GAAP), Federal Deposit Insurance Corporation (FDIC), and the Internal Revenue Service (IRS), as well as health inspectors, lending laws, local ordinances, and zoning regulations. There isn't room in today's business climate to "fake it until you make it."

ASK FOR HELP

When the audit was presented to me, I didn't know how to decipher the information, so I did the only thing I could do. I asked for help. I created a presidential advisory team that met once a month to discuss finances. On the team were nine people with different backgrounds. Some of them had experience in finance or accounting, others were nonfinancial people who used the data to make decisions. This team would meet, look at the information, discuss it and make recommendations based on their education, experience, and insight. This allowed me to make good decisions based on information that no one had ever taught me to understand.

The first thing I learned was that the most important number could be found on page three. (For other organizations, the number may be on a different page, so don't take my advice too literally.) Once I found that number, I checked to see if it had parentheses around it. If so, it was a negative number. That was bad. If not, it was a positive number, and that was good. Soon I became a financial expert and could flip open the audit and look for the parentheses, though obviously that wasn't enough information to make informed decisions.

So I learned that I had to depend on my team. I had to be healthy enough to say, "I don't understand this," or "I don't know that; can you explain it to me?"

I learned to bring different kinds of people together.

For example, staff members at a church don't regularly attend board meetings; however, it makes sense for the accountant to meet with the financial committee, so she can respond to questions. Likewise, when a salesperson wants to sell a church a new security or investment plan, rather than meeting only with the pastor, everyone involved in finances at the church should be invited.

The Bible says that there is safety in the multitude of good counsel. Proverbs 15:22 says, "Refuse good advice and watch your plans fail; take good counsel and watch them succeed" (MSG). This is especially true in the case of financial counsel. One trusted and knowledge-able advisor isn't enough; seek financial advice from several qualified people with different backgrounds and personalities to ensure unbiased feedback.

As leaders, we are always involved in the decisions, but the role we play may change when it comes to financial or legal matters. For example, when there is a big real estate deal at the church, we're part of that decision; but we're there as a visionary, not a pragmatist. There's nothing wrong with a visionary being involved, but at the end of the deal the pragmatists will rule. They are the ones to fill out the paperwork and double check the calculations that go on the forms. We can enhance our own abilities immediately by getting other people to help us.

We need to encourage the people who work for us to come up with multiple solutions and then strategies for implementing each of those solutions. Demanding this kind of information and strategic planning from the people who work for us is one way to develop them as leaders. This is a practical example of how we can help raise the ceiling. By expecting more information from them than they are currently giving, we can help them raise their leadership ceilings.

MORE THAN DATA

Some of our advisors may be paid, and some not paid; the same principles that apply to selecting ladder holders also apply to the advisors we select. But it is important to maintain a balance, too. When the organization reaches a certain size, having an accountant on staff is necessary. As we grow larger, it becomes important to have a paid, independent accountant available for external audits and some financial reporting.

We want to find a balance between people we are close enough so that we can pick up the phone and call for a quick question and those who are distant enough to have an independent, outside opinion.

Some leaders say, "We can't afford the financial or legal help we need." If an organization can't afford it, the leaders shouldn't be doing it because they will pay for it one way or another. Spending $50,000 a year for good legal or financial advice isn't much to pay if it could ultimately save us from five million dollars in penalties or, worse, jail time.

Good advisors give us four items in this order:

- *Data.* They tell us the information.

- *Implications of the data.* They explain what the data means to us. It is the context that helps us create meaning out of the information.

- *Recommendations on the implications.* The advisor believes this is the best advice she can offer us based on the information and its meaning.

- *Strategies for the recommendations.* These are the who, what, why, how and when of implementing a chosen recommendation.

FINANCIAL DON'TS

Don't let advisors decide. A leader should always be the one to make the final decision. The information should be presented and even discussed by a team of financial counselors, but we should never abdicate our decision-making power. If we don't have the information we need, we can request that the advisors do more research, get new advisors or ask more questions.

Regardless, we must take responsibility for the decision. Vision and ultimate decision-making are two things a leader should never delegate.

Don't get compromised. Many leaders start out as principled decision-makers, but in an effort to make numbers look more appealing to their stakeholders, they begin to make decisions based on situations. Don't let circumstances guide financial decisions. Always make decisions based on principle, regardless of the immediate consequences. The long-term consequences of situational decision-making will always be worse than the immediate cost.

Don't try to do everything. If I can help leaders understand one thing, it would be that they don't have to do everything. This is especially true in areas where they may be ill equipped to do the job, such as financial management.

DO WHAT YOU DO BEST

There is a big difference between understanding your church, ministry or business and understanding the "business" that allows it to function financially and legally. Often, church and organizational leaders are not equipped to direct these functions. As a visionary, you may understand your product or service, customers or constituents and have a clear view of the future—that's what has allowed you to climb the leadership ladder as high as you have. However, as your organizations scales, the gaps in your knowledge will become more pronounced as you focus on the things that matter.

Your lack of education and experience in this area makes you a liability rather than an asset. In these cases, the best information comes from trusted advisors who aren't afraid to teach you what they already know. They are ultimately the ones who can provide you with the information you need to make the best decisions and ascend to the next rung without an unexpected disaster.

CHAPTER 11
DELEGATION

Surround yourself with the best people you can find,
delegate authority, and don't interfere.
—Ronald Reagan, 40th President of the United States

As a college president, I was like most leaders. I was in the unenviable position of being able to choose my own pain. Specifically, that meant that when an important project came up, I could choose to do it myself, or I could delegate it to someone else. Either option caused me pain.

Doing it myself typically meant working long hours and letting other responsibilities slip as I plodded my way through the task alone. After doing this a few times, it didn't take long for me to realize that I couldn't do everything by myself. Other aspects of my job—aspects that only I could attend to—didn't get the attention they needed as I focused my energy on the project. And my family suffered because I had to spend more time at work.

But at the time, delegating jobs to other people didn't seem like a better option. When I did everything myself, I knew it would get done exactly the way I wanted it. But if I delegated that responsibility, I had no assurance of the outcome. There were more questions than answers. *What if she doesn't do the job the way I would? What if her performance isn't up to my standards? What if she completely fails and I still have to do it?* Not only would I still have to get the job done on time, but now I would have even less time in which to do it.

That's why I say it was an unenviable position. I could choose between the pain of doing it myself and the pain of delegating it.

DELEGATING DIFFICULTIES

As our organizations grow, there comes a time when we learn that we can't do it all ourselves. For leaders who are used to being in charge, this means a new type of pain: the pain of delegating.

Leaders are accustomed to being in control, so delegating can be hard for us. The more I delegate, the more out of control I am, and the greater the opportunity there is for something to go wrong. Delegating can cause conflict, disappointment and discouragement; ultimately, it could still mean that I end up doing it myself.

That's why we often hear leaders say, "If I want it done right, I'll just do it myself." We like the feeling of control that comes from knowing that we rise or fall based on our own actions. Yet control can camouflage pain, the pain associated with doing it ourselves. We can't do it all alone, other aspects of our work and family life suffer, and we never live up to our perfectionist tendencies.

We may choose to go it alone, yet when we're in the situation, we complain there is never anyone to help us. The truth is, people are willing to help us; we just have to be willing to go through the pain of delegating. When a leader continues to hold on long after he should have let go, it is a good sign that he is drowning. Only drowning people have a death grip, so if people don't want to give up, it could mean they are drowning.

Avoid people who can't let go. Drowning victims will try to take their rescuers down with them in their desperate struggle to hang on. Leaders who haven't learned to delegate are needy and clinging. They will drown themselves through their inability to delegate to others.

All leaders have the same opportunity I had as president of the college; we can trade one kind of pain for another. Either we do tasks ourselves, or we delegate them.

PAIN THRESHOLD DETERMINES HEIGHT

The more pain you can handle as a leader, the higher you will go. By learning to delegate and surviving the associated pain, we widen our bases and expand our horizons. For example, if I am the only person who can approve check requests, I must go through each request before a check can be issued. Occasionally, a vendor needs a check immediately to ensure a discount or certain delivery deadline. In order for that vendor to get his check, I must stop whatever I am doing and review the request, authorize it and then ask the accountant to prepare the check.

I could delegate this responsibility to my assistant. If I do so, I know he is likely to make mistakes. Some of those mistakes could be costly. But if I don't delegate, I will continue to be interrupted to review check requests, even while I am working on more important things.

Leaders will only grow to the threshold of their pain. In other words, I won't allow my assistant to review check requests unless I am willing to go through the pain of teaching him and watching him fail. If I make it through that pain, I have someone else to review the check requests, and I no longer have to deal with interruptions. I can do more and do it with greater concentration now that I have delegated another responsibility.

If we insist on staying in control, our organizations can grow no larger than our own abilities. However, if we learn to delegate and then do it over and over again, we expand the base of our organization. Of course, the only way to grow the organization is to expand the base.

THE ANTIDOTE TO PAIN

The solution to the pain of delegation is the three Ds we discussed in Part I of this book: Discover, Develop and Deploy. I *discover* that Amber has many of the leadership qualities we discussed in Part I of this book. I decide that I will *develop* her as a leader and spend a lot of time helping her grow. But I can't stop there. At some point I have to stop developing and start trusting that she is ready to take on her own responsibilities. I need to start delegating things to Amber; I need to *deploy* her as a leader. The last thing I want to do is raise a leader and then allow her gifts to stagnate. Yet that is why many good people have been forced to leave their churches or businesses; the leader was not willing to deploy them. As leaders, we have to remember that the more responsibility we delegate, the higher we can go.

CHAPTER 12
EXECUTION

*To me, ideas are worth nothing unless executed. They are
just a multiplier. Execution is worth millions.*
—Steve Jobs, co-founder and former CEO of Apple

I was riding in a car with a pastor of a large and prestigious church.
We were talking about the growth he was experiencing when he
suddenly interrupted the conversation. "Excuse me, but I need to call
the church. Your comment reminded me of something." He then
used his cell phone to call the worship leader to make sure a detail
was being handled for Sunday's service.

We continued the conversation, but soon it happened again. "Pardon
me, I just remembered that we were supposed to respond to the
zoning board today with some information it needs to consider our
rezoning request. Let me just call the office, and make sure they
remembered to take care of it." As we drove, our conversation was
interrupted many times while the pastor made phone calls to follow
up on one item or another.

Some might think the pastor was disorganized or he was trying to micromanage his people. I might have thought the same thing, but I've seen the same symptoms with many other leaders. The pastor was trying to make sure his people followed through with what they promised to do. He was following up to see that his team had done their jobs, that they had executed the plan. I see this kind of behavior in organizations all the time. After all is said and done, more is said than done.

If leadership is about anything, it is about managing expectations. Our job is to minimize the distance between expectations and reality. The closer we can bring them together, the less conflict there will be. The best way to make sure that expectations and reality match is to communicate the details clearly and concretely.

Like the pastor in the situation above, my clients often tell me that nothing is happening in their organizations because there is a lack of implementation. They wake up in the middle of the night asking themselves, *I wonder if that got done? Did that letter go out in today's mail? I hope she made that phone call. I wonder who is handling the details of the event. Did they get the contribution statements out on time?* When the leader is out of the office, these kinds of questions swarm like mosquitoes that must constantly be swatted by phoning the office to see if they are being handled.

The leader doesn't have the peace of mind that he can delegate the details to someone else to finish. Instead, he is surrounded by people who say yes because they want the credit, but they fail to follow through. These people push the details down to the next level and hope they get done. This issue highlights the gap between the senior leader and the next level of leadership.

INGREDIENTS OF EXECUTION

When in a meeting, before moving from one agenda item to another, answer the question, "Who does what by when?" If this question doesn't get answered, the job is not going to get done. So, when I lead meetings, I always ask *who* is going to do *what* before I move on. Then I find out *when* they will get it done.

The when is an important part of this equation. We can't forget the when. If I say, "Chris, get back to me as soon as possible," I already know that my "as soon as possible" is sooner than his "as soon as possible." When I say to someone, "Be there early," I already know that my "early" is earlier than his "early." Unless we put a specific *when* with the *who* and the *what*, we will most likely be disappointed when our expectations do not align with reality. A vague "when" is the same as not having a "when" at all.

Most of us have interviewed for jobs. At the end of a meeting, the interviewer has four choices as to how to follow up. He can say:

- "I'll get back to you."

- "I'll get back to you next week."

- "I'll get back to you next Wednesday."

■ "I'll get back to you next Wednesday at 10:00."

As the person who is waiting to hear back, which one would you prefer? I know I would prefer the one that was most specific. It is clear as to what will happen and when it will happen. But what if the interviewer said instead, "I will get back to you soon." Suppose another job came up on Tuesday, should I take it or not? Maybe my definition of "soon" was Monday.

Most high-impact leaders are shouting, "Just get it done. Make it happen!" But it is easier to make it happen when we know who is supposed to do what by when. John Maxwell says, "People don't do what you expect; people do what you inspect." Knowing who is to do it and when it is supposed to be done makes it easy for us to inspect and hold them accountable if it doesn't get done.

The slogan for the Nike shoe company is, "Just do it!" If leaders want to see results and avoid conflict, then I say, "Ask who will be doing what by when, and then inspect what you expect."

CHAPTER 13
FUTURE THINKING

*The opportunity of a lifetime must be seized
during the lifetime of the opportunity.*
—Leonard Ravenhill, English evangelist

It was like every monthly leadership meeting at every other mid-sized church or Christian non-profit across America. First the pastor or CEO prayed and offered a brief devotional. Then the CFO gave a report on cashflow and budgets, cautioning team leaders to keep an eye on their year-to-date spending. The director of development reported on the latest fundraising campaign, and the HR director explained the new team training that was being rolled out to the staff. Next month the meeting will be the same, with some slight differences.

While it may sound dull, the problem isn't that the meetings are dull. (Though they probably are.) The problem is with the focus of the meeting. These meetings almost entirely look at the past. They report what has been and what is, not what is coming up. When they do discuss future issues, the issues are almost entirely those facing the organization in the next twelve months. Leaders need to spend less time looking at the past and more time anticipating the future. In this chapter, I would like to explore why this is the case, and some of the questions leaders need to ask as they look forward.

FUTURE PLANNING

The world I was trained to lead in doesn't exist anymore. Pastors weren't taught how to prepare a sermon using multimedia, yet large screens projecting graphics, maps, Bible verses and videos often overshadow today's pulpits. Using a song, dance or short drama to set up the sermon topic is also popular in many churches. Some services are designed entirely for online worshipers, and others cater to those who want a liturgical service that reflects historic traditions—both occurring in the same church! The way I was trained to preach, teach, administrate and counsel isn't effective in today's church.

Likewise, in the business world, executives are expected to be conversant not only on the details of their bottom line, but also on issues in broader culture that may seem totally unrelated to their business, such as social justice, climate change and sustainability. They must be willing to engage with constituents on social media, master new technology, build virtual teams across time zones and maintain diversity in the workplace. It's a brave new world.

Suppose I send my first child off to kindergarten today. What will life be like for him when he graduates high school? For adults living today, a major rite of passage was buying a car in high school and moving away from home to go to college. Many experts predict that children born today will never own a car, instead preferring autonomous ride-sharing technology that will be ubiquitous in the next decade. As the coronavirus pandemic of 2020 taught us, higher education can be brought almost entirely online with minimal disruption to academic progress, making the rituals surrounding "moving away to go to college" a novelty instead of an expectation. In twenty years, will e-mails still be around? Television? What subjects will they study in high school or college? What jobs are here today that won't be here then? Will our children and grandchildren even leave their homes to go to work?

In my book *Futuring: Leading Your Church Into Tomorrow*, I suggest this is the kind of thinking that needs to be done inside our churches and organizations. We need to have extended planning sessions to get our teams to think creatively about what the organizations we lead will look like years from now. Fifteen years is too far out. I recommend teams start by looking at the next three to five years. Divide the leaders into groups, and give them questions to investigate. Ask them to report their findings in three months.

These questions will get them started:

- Over the next three to five years, how will our organization's constituents or customers change demographically?

- Will we have more male or female constituents?

- Which age group will grow the fastest? Why?

- What will the ethnicity, socioeconomic factors and education of our constituents be like in three years?

- How will the neighborhoods and communities we are reaching look?

- What developments are planned that we don't know about?

- Is there a plan to build a Walmart, a new school, or a low-income subsidized apartment complex on land nearby?

- Is there a highway planned that could come through the parking lot and take three acres of our property?

- How will traffic flow change based on new construction patterns?

Some of this local information is available from city hall, the Chamber of Commerce, or other local business bureaus. Other data is available from online services that specialize in market data and predictive analytics. Other pieces of information can be taken from corporate cues. For example, if McDonald's has recently moved into the neighborhood, we can assume that the corporation believes the neighborhood will be steady for the next few years. If the local McDonald's franchise builds a playground, corporate research probably shows there are a lot of growing families nearby.

Is the local school board considering a new school building? If so, educators are planning for growth in the next five to ten years. Is the school an elementary, middle, or high school? What does that tell us about growth in this area? Are there water or electrical lines being run to a certain location? Has a developer filed plans for a subdivision even though work hasn't begun on the land?

Answering these questions and others like them can help us understand how the needs of our constituents and customers might be changing in the near future.

Suppose our team members at a church come back in a few months and have found information that suggests the community around the church will be increasingly Latino. They've also learned that a subsidized housing complex will be built on the next block. Knowing this information, we can make decisions about our ministries and programming. For example, who on the staff speaks Spanish? Have we considered an English as a second language ministry? Should we add a Spanish-speaking worship service? What other services can we offer? Should we consider adding a daycare for working mothers?

Someone once said, "Opportunities are never postponed; they're lost forever." We will miss opportunities if we are not intentionally planning. Leaders need to spend more time thinking about the future and less time thinking about the past. The only thing we can do about the past is learn from it; even so, for those lessons to be valuable, they have to be applied to the future.

FUTURING LEADERS

Futuring leaders forecast trends, envision scenarios and help to create the desired future. Futuring leaders are vision driven. They say things like, "Where are we going? What are we going to do?" not, "Where have we been?" They look through the windshield while they drive, not the rearview mirror.

If we attend a meeting led by a futuring leader, the time will be spent on things that are coming up rather than things that have already been. A futuring leader intentionally applies the lessons from the past to future activities. Her whole way of thinking and talking is focused on the future.

A future focus has implications far beyond just planning and strategy. It even affects how we develop people. For example, if Bart messes up, many leaders would get on him for his mistakes. A futuring leader uses language in a different way, saying instead, "Bart, the next time you do this. . . ." His whole vocabulary is about the future.

Using the example of the leadership meeting above, a financial person who works for a futuring leader won't bring only reports to the monthly staff meeting. Instead, he will also bring projections. He knows that financial and strategic planning go arm in arm. Likewise, when it comes time to talk about fundraising, the development director will spend less time on the recent campaign performance and more time on how learning from the campaign will impact future plans. The HR director will explore employment trends and help team leaders understand what the worker of tomorrow will need to do her job.

The future opens up possibilities. Futuring leaders are exciting to be around because they always see the opportunities, but we can't be futuring leaders alone. We must also take time to help our teammates learn to be future gazers and future planners.

PAST LEADERS VS. FUTURE LEADERS

The leaders who got us to this point may not be the ones who carry us into the future. This is one of the hardest lessons to learn. The people who got our church from 100 to 200 members may not be the ones that take us from 200 to 300. People who got our organization from five staff members to fifteen may not be the ones who take us from fifteen to thirty staff members. Let me say it this way: Our new leaders will rarely be our old leaders. It's not that they're incapable of leading; it's that they are incapable of seeing the organization any differently than when they came in.

We need to recruit future-thinking leaders to go with us. We need people who can envision the future. Some of our original leaders won't be able to take the journey, so we need to plan for how we disengage them as leaders. This transition can be difficult, but it is necessary. As leaders, we need to have our minds on the future and have the activities to back it up.

PART III

THE TRANSITION

INTRODUCTION

You had the vision—you knew where you wanted to go, and you climbed faithfully and finally reached the top of your ladder, achieving most or all of your goals. After you've reached the top of the ladder, you will likely face transition. After all, in life nothing is permanent.

For example, one day I realized I had climbed the ladder of success as the president of a growing college. For fourteen years, I had dreamed and worked hard as I ascended that golden ladder. I loved the people, the work, the challenges and the excitement of going up each rung. One day, however, something changed. (I write "one day," but something had been going on for months until the day I became aware.)

Who moved my ladder? This isn't where I want to stay, I thought. As I was to learn, many leaders are or have been exactly where I stood that

117

day. Who moved our ladders? Who changed things? Who took away the excitement? The joy? The challenge?

The truth is, where I stood on my ladder was exactly where I had wanted to go—at least it was when I started up that particular ladder. What I had to face—and so do many of us—is that it may appear as if someone has moved our ladder. The excitement, joy and challenge dissipate. We look over our shoulder and realize where we were when we first felt those giddy emotions and rushed up those rungs. Those were the days when we jumped out of bed every morning. Even at night when we put our weary bodies to bed, we felt as if we had accomplished something. We knew we were moving in the right direction; we had climbed a little higher on the ladder.

When that level of enthusiasm begins to drain, here's the reality we have to face: No one has moved our ladder. It's in exactly the same place it has always been. We have changed. We climbed the ladder— and it may have been the right one—but it's no longer the preferred or fulfilling one. At least, that was my experience.

Some may have climbed high on ladders, and as they neared the top they said, "Oh, this isn't really where I wanted to go." In my case, it hadn't been that my ladder was leaned against the wrong wall; how- ever, it would have been the wrong wall had I continued to stay. My ladder had moved. That is, my vision had changed.

One day, I surveyed the world from my ladder. The passion had diminished. I didn't hate my ladder or what I was doing. It felt, well, a bit predictable, even a little boring. "I've done this before," I said.

What's wrong with me? That's the question most of us ask ourselves when the thrill of our jobs subsides. Surely, there was something wrong with me. If something had become defective, I had to figure out what part malfunctioned, fix it and move on. As I pondered that question, I realized that I had been standing in about the same place for several months. Activities had not stopped—I had set things up so that no one noticed my standing still. But I noticed.

More important, off and on for months I searched and beat up on myself for having lost my cutting-edge enthusiasm. Somewhere in the process, however, I slowly admitted that I wasn't the problem. The problem was the ladder.

What had happened to the beautiful, wonderful ladder I had been climbing? Where was the excitement I had felt as I slowly ascended? Where was the inner contentment and joy? Why was there no constant excitement as I stared at the next rung?

What's happened? Who had moved my golden ladder? Was it time to find a new ladder? Was it time to hang on, grit my teeth, and just keep doing what I'd been doing for more than a decade? Or was it time to climb off my ladder and find a new one?

It was a time of transition—but it took me weeks to accept that fact.

Some people have to move. They're laid off, fired or told, "Find a different job." They're forced to make changes. But how do we go about making transitions when all is going well? When we're successful? When we've achieved more than we ever dreamed? When our friends and critics still applaud our achievements?

I had climbed higher on the ladder than anyone had expected. After I reached the top rung, I realized something: I had gone as far as I could on this ladder. I had to think about where I was and where I wanted to go next. If it was time to switch ladders, which one do I climb now? Was it time to relax, rest, stand and survey what I had done and enjoy it?

Most leaders face that situation sometime in their careers—and some more than once. It's not a comfortable place in which to stand.

I began my search for resources to assist me in my transitional decision-making. Here are some of the issues I struggled with:

- What is going on?

- Why was I excited and scared at the same time?

- What were the critical questions I need to ask?

- What were the essential ingredients?

- What about a successor?

To my amazement and dismay, I found little information available. That's what Part III of this book is all about. You may be just beginning the climb, or nearing the top of your ladder, but sooner or later you will make a transition. What are the inner promptings that will guide your move? How will you discern timing? Who will walk with you in the process? And where will you go next? I will share some of my own journey of transition, along with practical insights I gathered in the process. The inevitable transition you will someday face does not need to be terrifying. It can be exhilarating and can position you for even greater heights of success on the next ladder God has given you to climb.

CHAPTER 14

DISCONTENT & DISCERNMENT

Restlessness is discontent, and discontent is the first necessity of progress.
—Thomas A. Edison, inventor and entrepreneur

My transition began with what I call godly discontent. I had worked hard to help the college move forward—and it had happened. I had met each goal and every challenge that confronted me. Instead of feeling joyful and excited, boredom set in.

Most leaders go after challenges—whether growing a church or developing an organization, adding staff, boosting productivity or increasing finances. When we've done that, we begin to feel like Alexander the Great. One legend says that once he had conquered the then-known world, he sat down and cried. He had no more worlds to conquer.

My world wasn't that vast or my accomplishments that great, but I had done more than I had set out to do. I'd stare at my desk calendar and sigh. "I've done all this before." For some, the discontent forces them to increase their activity and struggle to recapture the thrill of success. For a short time, I tried to do just that. I thought the answer was doing more. After a few weeks, I realized that "more" didn't mean greater enjoyment or excitement. "More" simply meant I was busier. How did I regain that enthusiasm? For weeks, I pondered my dilemma. I didn't talk about it, because I didn't know how to talk about it.

That was the beginning of a godly discontent—even though I didn't know to label it that way.

There were things I did—and did well—but something within me whispered, *I don't want to continue doing the same things again and again.* As I listened to my inner groanings, I admitted that I didn't want to do more administration. I was tired of fundraising. Dealing with staff issues began to tire me. I didn't want to do conflict management any more. I didn't want to schedule more meetings or breakfasts or accept more preaching opportunities. I cringed at the thought of having to conduct one more job interview. I didn't want to deal with the financial aspects of our school—even though we were in a healthy situation. Those were typical of the things I had to face that I didn't want to do anymore.

Inner boredom. That's what afflicted me, and once I admitted it to myself, I kept it hidden from others. "I can handle all the job demands in my sleep," I said aloud. I could do those things—and I had been doing them for fourteen years—but I just didn't want to do them any longer. As long as I focused on what was wrong with me, I got nowhere. Once I opened myself to the possibility of God, I knew I was moving in the right direction.

What if my discontent is from God? What if this is the first step toward disengaging myself from the old to prepare me for the new? That's when I understood the concept of godly discontent. It meant I was all right, and no matter how much effort I forced, I would grow even more disenchanted.

I had to switch ladders, but I didn't know which ladder to grab. There were many of them out there, and I could have started climbing any of them.

This is what makes ladder transition even more challenging than beginning at the bottom of the ladder. When you're at the bottom, your options are fairly limited—whether it is the number of roles you are qualified to take or the number of organizations recruiting you. When you've reached the top of a ladder, however, others notice. You may receive offers you're not even looking for, and you will have to choose among multiple good opportunities.

Before I could move to a new ladder, I had to be certain I didn't want to stay in my present position. Almost every day I argued with myself. At first, I was too scared to seriously contemplate leaving. I had worked hard, earned the respect of my peers, and—for the first time in my life—had brought financial stability into my life. I could stay in my present position until my retirement.

Or could I?

Every choice held risk—it was risky to leave my present position, it was risky to stay. If I resigned, should I leave right away or wait another year? How long did I plan before I took action?

DISCERNING GOD'S WILL

I believe the discontent I was feeling was from God, and if it was, it stands to reason that He was using it to redirect me to a different ladder. While the discontent may have indicated that it was time to change ladders, it did not give me much direction for what the next ladder should be. Where does God's will fit into this realm of transition? As I pondered, I was reminded of leadership expert Tim Elmore's four ways in which God speaks to us.

First is the thunderbolt. This is like Paul being knocked down on the road to Damascus or God speaking three times in a dream to Samuel. Can God speak that way? Absolutely. Does God often speak that way? Probably not.

Second is the call from birth. In the Old Testament, there were people called Nazirites, such as Samuel and Samson. In the New Testament era, John the Baptist probably fits into that category. From the time of their births, their parents dedicated them to God's service. For those children, choice was no option. They grew up knowing what God wanted and expected of them.

Third is a slow, growing awareness. It's not an immediate reaction and may take many years to unfold. It's like a latent talent. It's there all along, but it's hidden deeply within until we discover its presence. When we are following the Holy Spirit's guidance, we have peace ruling in our hearts. When we try something new, do it well and enjoy it, that's a strong indication of God's plan gradually unfolding in our lives.

Fourth is that we see open doors. I can always walk out of a room but I can't always walk into a room. I can always say no but I can't always say yes. If a door opens to me, I believe my responsibility is to peek inside. I may not know if it's God's will, but investigating the open door won't hurt.

For me, God's will has always been a fuzzy issue. I can't boil it down like some people who have an instant, easy formula. How He speaks to others is different from the way He speaks to me. I don't know a great deal about God's will, but I have learned to know the wavelength or frequency on which the Spirit communicates with me.

As we reflect on God's movement in our lives, here's a good question to ask: Do I know how God speaks to me? (Many people don't know the answer.)

The tendency for most of us—and I'm no exception—is that we always want to know or at least to understand God's will and ways. I've heard so many people quote Romans 8:28 (NASB): "And we know that all things work together for good to those who love God, to those who are the called according to His purpose." Then they add, "Someday we'll understand." Maybe we won't—not ever. When we're seeking God's will, we keep saying, "Show me. Tell me. Speak to me." If we really knew, we wouldn't be walking by faith.

The Danish theologian Soren Kierkegaard insisted that the highest good is to find our vocation (or calling) in life. He spoke of discerning God's will through using personal experience (growing awareness) and our convictions (open doors or obvious opportunities).

For me, once I sensed the direction God was taking me, I needed to take Kierkegaard's leap of faith—to jump into the unknown—and trust God's hands to grab me. I lead with my heart, and my head has to follow. This isn't the method for everyone, but it's how I sense God at work in *my* life.

Here's one more way for people to see the Holy Spirit at work in their lives. I ask them to review their own spiritual journey. Look at all the significant moments in their lives. As they do so, I urge them to ask themselves:

- Where are God's footprints in my life?

- What divine patterns can I see?

- How does the Lord speak most often to me?

- What were the last three major decisions I made? What were the common factors in all of them?

Where does living on the edge by faith play a role? There's an old saying, "If we're not living on the edge, we're taking up too much room."

That means we need to keep moving. The edge needs to become edgier. There is no such place where we can stand and say, "This is the edge," because the edge is always extending itself. Otherwise, eventually the edge becomes our comfort zone.

CHAPTER 15
VALUES & PASSION

When your values are clear to you, making decisions becomes easier.
—Roy Disney, co-founder of the Walt Disney Company

As I moved forward in my internal transition of identifying my godly discontent and discerning God's will, I also asked myself: *What are my core values? Who is the quintessential Samuel Chand? If anyone probed deeply enough, what values would they see that truly guide my life?*

Some things are important to us at our core—our inner being—and others matter because they're important to our culture, our corporation, our community or our family. It's not always easy to distinguish between core values and important concerns. It's easy to convince ourselves the values that are important to our organizations or our churches are those we love and must, thus, be of equal importance to us. When relationships tend to go bad, it's often because of a confusion between core values and important concerns.

Increasingly, I saw that my value was as simple as the words of Jesus. He said that the first command was to love God totally and the second "is like it," that is, it is of equal importance: "Love your neighbor as yourself" (Matthew 22:38, NIV).

I thought of it this way: If I zealously do what I can to enable others to look good—to be their best—isn't that one way of fulfilling the words of Jesus? If I help a pastor, I help the whole church; if I help a CEO, I'll help the whole organization.

I also realized how true this was with a little illustration. Suppose God said to me, "Make a choice. If you enter the first door, you'll find twenty pastors in there waiting for your help. If you take the second door, you'll face twenty thousand Christians. Choose which group you want, and I'll be with you."

That decision didn't require any reflection. I would answer, "I'll go for the twenty." That made me realize my core value.

There were other values, and, of course, the one above is only one of them. But to know—to acknowledge those core values—means we have to be in touch with ourselves, with our inner selves. For some people, it's extremely difficult to probe deeply.

The other problem I saw in the matter of core values is that some try to claim too many. My guess—based on my experience in working with leaders and examining my own heart—is that, at most, most of us have three to five core values. If we truly ponder this, we'll probably cut them down to three.

How do we discover those core values? We do a great deal of soul searching—including checking on our own motives. We ask ourselves, *What do I value most?* We relentlessly probe: *What do I care about? What do I dream about? When I daydream, what are the values?*

All of us have strong needs for acceptance, love and affirmation. They're stronger in some people than they are in others, and they're certainly part of the core issues we struggle with.

IDENTIFYING YOUR PASSION

Who am I? Everyone asks that question (or should) eventually in life—and it's an important issue to grapple with. A second question, not asked as often, follows: *What is my life purpose?*

Years ago, I first asked myself that question and stayed with it until I had an answer. I could have asked it in many ways:

- What is my life purpose?

- What am I gifted to do?

- What are my greatest abilities, and how do I use them?

- What produces the best results?

- Where do I find the greatest fulfillment?

Instead, I focused on the question about life purpose: What do I do best? When and how am I the most effective in my life?

Running programs and institutions bored me, but one aspect of my work still intrigued me. That one part of my work—and it was fairly small—brightened my worst days. As I noted earlier, I believed that one of my core values was to follow the great commandment—to love God and love my neighbor. But what was the specific way that I was wired to love my neighbor? Where was the intersection of my values and my passion? (i.5)

Due to my role, I sometimes functioned as a leadership consultant. I want to help leaders reach their highest potential, I thought. I want to serve leaders as their dream releaser. My vision is to help others succeed.

I realized that almost every pastor I met or CEO I consulted with, I was building them up, encouraging them, and helping them succeed. Dream releasing was ongoing and always new. Each consultation brightened my day.

What does that mean? I asked myself.

Even though I wasn't aware, the more consulting I did, the more enthusiastic I became. This sideline forced me to read more books and articles and listen to more recordings and lectures than I ever had before. Except for my days as a college student, I couldn't remember when I had felt such a driving zeal to know more and to understand better.

I didn't have any magic moment or instant stroke of enlightenment, but I gradually came to realize that I'm a dream releaser. I love to help others succeed. Others have dreams but don't seem to know how to make those dreams turn into reality. God has given me the ability to help them release those dreams.

That pushed me to ask, Okay, how do I know if I'm being effective at releasing others' dreams? I looked at what I had already accomplished at the college. My ideas had worked and we had developed a great school—not perfect but good. We had come a long way in the years I had been there.

What is God doing in my life? I asked. What are my gifts? What is being affirmed most by me? Where do I find the greatest fulfillment?

The life-purpose question doesn't stop there—it's something we must continue to push and probe. Once I answered one question, another popped up and then another.

What makes me pound the table with passion? What makes me weep? What brings me joy? What kind of interactions enable me to walk away saying to myself, Yes! Yes. I have a sense of fulfillment?

Only in looking back was I able to realize it, but that's when the first seeds of godly dissatisfaction were sown. I wanted to be able to spend ninety-five percent of my time dream releasing and five percent doing other things. How could I make that possible?

When we discover the right direction, passion returns. Until then, it's as if we've been living in a dead zone. We're bored or uneasy, and nothing fills us with deep fulfillment and joy.

Here's a question leaders need to ask when they move from one position to another: Am I passionate enough right now that I can envision staying at this job for the rest of my professional life? Or is this only temporary? If it's only temporary, what are my motives for saying yes to the job?

In my case, I don't consider what I do as a job. It is, of course, and I get paid. But I think of what I do in terms of personal fulfillment and satisfaction that I have helped other people.

When we're passionate about our work, we may not be in the right place, but it's a good indication that we're moving in the right direction.

Like everyone, I have the capacity for self-delusion or self-deception. What if I was wrong? What if this was a mistake or a temporary dissatisfaction? What if this was a burnout situation and not truly godly dissatisfaction? What if being a dream releaser wasn't the ladder God wanted me to climb?

It took a few weeks of internal struggle for me to become fairly confident I was moving in the right direction. Once I had a sense of where I thought I wanted to go, my first step was to seek counsel.

CHAPTER 16
WISE COUNSEL

The way of fools seems right to them, but the wise listen to advice.
—Proverbs 12:15 (NIV)

B efore we take any action in switching from one ladder to another, we need to seek counsel from others. Although I had vacillated, I knew it was time to move beyond my own frame of reference. I needed to talk to other leaders who not only understood transitions but who had also made them.

Many of us aren't good at opening up to others. We feel we can handle it alone. Or we may be too ashamed to admit that we don't know how to handle our own lives. Many of us, because of our own inner insecurities, are ambivalent about opening ourselves up to anyone else. Even if we want to open up, it's not easy. When we speak with those who can help us the most, it's as if we expect them to read our minds because we can't say the words, "Help me. Help me think this thing through."

People have offered excuses for not opening up, but I'm convinced that God intended for us to share our burdens with others. Scripture says, "Where there is no counsel, the people fail; but in the multitude of counselors, there is safety" (Proverbs 11:14, NKJV).

The point is that unless we open up and benefit from the wisdom of others, we're apt to make unwise decisions. I didn't want to make the mistake of not listening to those with a different perspective. Once I made the decision to seek counsel, my first questions were: *Whom do I ask? Who will be the most helpful?* Talking to the wrong people could frustrate or discourage me. I needed to focus on those who had the experience and expertise to offer insight.

To prepare for sharing my situation, I sat at my desk and made a profile of the people I wanted to talk to about leaving the college. Because I wanted totally objective responses, I decided to eliminate anyone who would be involved in or affected by my decision.

I want to make it clear that my wife, Brenda, would be the most adversely affected if things went wrong. But we believed in the biblical concept that a husband and a wife become one (see Genesis 2:24; Matthew 19:6). She functioned not only as part of me but as my sounding board throughout the whole process. I talked with her about some of the inner issues that I was not able to talk about with others.

We don't go around and ask advice of anyone who will listen to us. We need to be selective about whom we ask. I had decided to talk only to those who could give me *professional* advice.

After I decided on the type of people I wanted to consult, I made my list—adding and subtracting names until I knew I had the people with whom I could talk freely. I ended up with fourteen names. One by one, I called and made appointments to spend time with them when they could carefully advise me.

I was going to climb a ladder I had never climbed before. I didn't know if it was securely planted or how high it would reach. Was I scared? Yes, I was. But I was also scared not to take the risk. Because I wanted to be sure I was taking the right risk, I asked other risk-takers for guidance.

I wasn't asking any of them to offer the traditional advice we get from the cautious or timid, such as, "I think you ought to pray more about this." "Don't you think you've got a good thing going now?" "Why leave now? Enjoy the fruit of your labors." "A lot of people get great ideas but they don't work out."

Although I had more than fourteen names on my original list, I didn't talk to all of them. By the time I had gone down the first half of my list, I realized I had received the guidance I needed.

The reason I didn't speak to all of those on my original list was that, even though they had good hearts, a few of them were stabilizers. They were good people, and I liked them, but I wasn't looking for stability; I wanted effectiveness. Too often, stability can get in the way. Consistency can thwart progress. I could go anywhere and be consistent.

One thing that stands out to me in retrospect is that not one of the individuals I spoke to cautioned me against leaving. Perhaps because they're all entrepreneurs at heart, they know the thrill of risk-taking. All of them had moved from security to embrace challenges.

They sensed I was moving in the right direction and at the right time. In consulting with those on my list, none of them challenged me to stay and make the college larger. By then, I was so far along in the process, I wasn't positive where I was going to end up, but I had to move from my comfortable ladder. I was convinced I couldn't remain the president much longer.

Just knowing I had wrestled with all the issues confirmed to me that I had done the right thing. I went to them because I needed outside people for perspective. The greatest need of a high-end leader is perspective. Good, helpful consultants offer us perspective—they help us see things in a different light. They ask the same questions we've already thought about—or should have.

To answer myself was one thing, but when someone I trust asks a question, stares at me and waits, I'll probably answer differently. I can lie to myself or convince myself of something I want to believe, but when someone else asks me, I'm more apt to get gut-level honest.

CHAPTER 17
DESIRES & TIMING

*There is a time for everything, and a season for every
activity under the heavens.*
—Ecclesiastes 3:1 (NIV)

Although I had identified my passion for helping other leaders
release their dreams, and I was confident that it was God's will
for me to move forward in pursuing this transition, I still faced big
questions that would help me determine *how* I would make the transition and what the new ladder would be that would take me to my
new destination.

What am I looking for? What do I need to find fulfillment?

After months of self-searching, I settled on four things.

1) Independence. I had never been independent before, and this
would be a new experience for me. No one would know—or care—if
I started to work at 6:00 a.m. or not until noon.

I had to ask myself: *Can I work independently?* I've functioned in structured situations all my life. Even when I was a pastor, there was some structure. I had hours at my discretion, but I had sermons to preach and lessons to teach, board meetings to conduct, visitation, baptisms, weddings and funerals.

I asked myself another question: *Do I like myself well enough to be alone all the time? Can I spend time with just me?* I had never done that. When I went to the office, there were people in and out all day. Some days I received forty phone calls. How would I react when I received only two in a week? No longer would anyone stop by my office and ask if I wanted coffee or if I wanted to go out for lunch.

I have a beautiful office in my home. It's nicer than the one I had in the school, but nobody comes to see me. I have never had one client there—and I won't.

Could I live with that amount of independence?

I can and I have, but it was an adjustment—and I knew it would be. Now I can truly say I love the quiet of my office.

2) Control. Do I need outside control, or do I have enough inner strength to traverse the journey with self-control? Do I have the self-discipline, accountability and integrity? Do I need outside energy or an authority figure to tell me what to do, or do I have what it takes? Can I get up in the morning if I don't have to keep office hours? Will I write that letter? Will I respond to that e-mail?

That one didn't trouble me because I've always been a self-starter.

3) Freedom. For me, this is different from independence. I had freedom at the college. I could come and go and the board fully understood—but I produced results. They didn't care so long as I brought in results.

I wanted to enjoy my freedom—my ability to choose the people to work with and to turn down those I didn't want to work with.

Here's an added dimension to the matter of freedom: Can I handle it when my income depends on the amount of freedom I demand? Freedom versus income. If I'm not careful, the need for income will destroy my freedom because I'll rush from project to project, afraid that I'll go bankrupt if I don't get the next job.

4) Structure. I needed some kind of structure, but what kind? I use that word to explain how I would organize myself. Once I'd decided that I was okay on the control issue, what kind of structure did I need to set up my business?

Immediately I set myself up with not-for-profit and for-profit corporations with board members. Would that be enough? How often would I need to meet with them? What kind of reports should I make?

During that time, one verse in the Bible gave me immense peace because I had sought God's will and believed I was doing the right thing: "The Lord will watch over your coming and going both now and forevermore" (Psalm 121:8, NIV).

A TIME FOR EVERYTHING

As I pondered the question of leaving, one central question kept hitting me: *Is this the right time to change ladders?* That's a big issue and the area where many leaders mess up. They leave too early, they leave before they've set everything in place or they leave too late.

Don't we all know of organizations where the leader has held on to power and refused to let go? The organization could have run more smoothly and perhaps moved in new and more challenging directions, but the person in charge couldn't step back.

Three years before I resigned, I became aware of my need for transition, but I couldn't do it then. I hadn't prepared for passing the baton. The college was going through accreditation renewal. We were going through federal financial aid re-approval. The board had not aligned itself. And most importantly, my successor wasn't ready.

I knew all along who should be my successor, but he still needed another year-and-a-half to two years to fit into the position. I had to make sure the timing was right for the transition to take place.

Then came decision time.

On Easter Sunday, 2003, my wife and I had been to Columbus, Georgia, where I preached at Solid Rock church. We were driving back to the south side of Atlanta where we live. We spoke about the situation of my resigning—and those minutes together turned into a powerful experience that is forever etched in my mind.

What made the conversation surprising was that Brenda and I had talked—in fact, I thought we had talked the issue to death and there was nothing else to say. Together we had looked at the transition from every possible angle. "What if this doesn't happen?" "What if that happens?" We figured on expenses and made budgets. We made what we called a fact budget and also a faith budget. I had learned long ago that God's numbers were always bigger than mine, so I wanted to think on two different levels.

Crawford Loritts, one of my fourteen mentors, taught me about a business plan and used the acronym of DOCTOR.

D = Directional

O = Objectives

C = Cash

T = Tracking

O = Overall Evaluation

R = Refinements

It was a good way for me to focus my thinking and find concrete ways to start fleshing out my thinking, and I started writing more.

For example "Cash" refers to the whole business, the overall picture: What do I see myself doing at the end of the day? How am I going to make adjustments? What's really my objective?

I assumed there was a good way to do a business plan. I wrote portions of such a plan, but not all of it. For example, I didn't write anything under Refinements. I'm not there yet. Cash? I sat down with my financial planner and went through the whole thing. We had already called a meeting with him, our CPA, Brenda, and me, and we planned the whole thing.

That Sunday afternoon, as we drove north on I-185, Brenda was quiet for a few seconds, then she said, "Let's go for it."

Just those words.

They were enough.

They rang like giant bells inside my heart. I knew it was right. And we made the decision right then—together.

CHAPTER 18
INTERNAL TRANSITION

We cannot become what we need by remaining what we are.
—John C. Maxwell

The process of transition includes both external and internal aspects—the practical details of moving from one ladder to another, and the mental, emotional and spiritual journey that each of us takes as we face transition. As I look back, I realize that I went through five internal stages in my transition.

Stage 1—Pre-contemplation

Stage 2—Contemplation

Stage 3—Darkness

Stage 4—Insight

Stage 5—Action

147

The only way I can explain it is to call the first step *pre-contemplation*. Pre-contemplation goes on when we know something ought to happen, but we don't know what. Something's not right, but we can't figure it out. This means we look at ourselves and wonder why we've failed or why we're not as committed to God or to our jobs as we used to be.

The second stage is *contemplation*. This is the stage of awareness. We know these facts: I'm not lazy. I'm not losing out with God. I'm not running away. We're not taking action, but we become aware that something will have to change.

Stage three is *darkness*. This is the most difficult place. I can't see to climb the next rung; I don't know how to go backward in all of the darkness. I knew I didn't want to be where I'd been, but I honestly didn't know where I wanted to go. We finally ask ourselves, *What do I do now?*

Even those who have an inkling of where they want to go next seem to have to go through the darkness. They catch a glimpse of what can be, but they don't see how it can come about.

"I can't go backward, and I don't know where forward is," I said. "It's not neutral; it's drifting." This is a stage of inner confusion. I was growing increasingly aware of the need for change, but I didn't know what to do or how to take the next step.

I called it a funk. The word comes from the name of Casmir Funk, a Polish biochemist who used his name to refer to dietary deficiencies.

It has come to refer to someone in a pessimistic state, someone who is unable to engage actively.

I didn't know where to go because I didn't know what to do. I didn't know how to go forward, and I wasn't ready to step backward. It's a terrible place—and *terrible* is the best word I can think of. Once we know where we want to go, we can face the challenge. We can take action.

Particularly as Christians, we groan and agonize as we cry out to God, "What is your will?" We truly want to know. We keep saying, "Show me what to do, and I'll do it." We also seek explanations or assurances.

I didn't know who I was then. I knew who I had been, and always thought I knew where I was going. I felt different, and it was as if the rules of the game had changed and no one had explained them to me. I wanted to move (remember, I'm action oriented) but with no sense of direction, what could I do? Do I step down a rung? Move up one rung or two? In many ways, this isn't the most crucial stage, but it's the most difficult because we have no sense of direction. All we know is that we don't want to be where we are now.

Stage four is *insight*. This can happen in an instant, or it can be like the first rays of light in the morning—they slowly push away the darkness. Sometimes it's knowing what to do without knowing how we know. It's as if the Holy Spirit whispers, "This is the way, walk in it." That also indicates that it's a way we've never been before.

Even with the insight, doubts may creep in. As soon as we get the insight, we argue with ourselves, *Can this be right? What if . . . ?*

We don't want to stay on the same ladder, but we don't know which ladder to climb. Or to use the image of climbing a mountain, we think we'll reach the summit—and we do—but then we see other mountains, and they beckon to us. They're higher mountains, and we realize they're where we want to go. As I stared at the various mountains, I thought, *They're not bad mountains, they're great mountains, but they aren't my mountains.*

This is also harder for people who can do many things. I had many job offers, and I never went out looking for any of them. One job offer was to become an administrator of a huge church; they would start me off at a high six-figure income—more money than I'd ever made in my life. It didn't even sound good.

As I continued to listen to God, I didn't know which ladder I was to switch to. I knew only two things.

First, I was going to leave this ladder.

Second, for several months, when I examined a new ladder, it wasn't the right one for me. In my case, it was an elimination process. That's exactly what happened in my life. *No, that's not for me,* I'd think. *No, that won't be long-term.* Questions also popped out, such as, *Will I do this for the rest of my life? If this is the last job I ever have, will I enjoy it?*

To use a different image, I saw bridges ahead. I'd lift my foot to step on one, and see the other side. I'd shake my head. *No, not that one either.* I kept moving along, scrutinizing every bridge. Some would take me across to the other side—but it wasn't the place I wanted to be.

I wasn't sure I knew where the other side was. I couldn't validate it in terms of concrete answers, but somehow I knew this was the right thing.

In my moment of insight, I had realized I wanted to be a consultant to pastors and leaders in large organizations. That was a risky decision. One of my first concerns was that I would be giving up a steady income. For many years, I had been able to count on a paycheck the first of the month.

In spite of this uncertainty, the insight persists and leads us to the fifth stage. This is the place of action, where an internal transition has external implications. This is where we hold the gun and pull the trigger. I climb down my ladder, my feet hit the ground, and I turn my back on the old ladder. I have to do that to be ready to climb a new one.

CHAPTER 19
EXTERNAL TRANSITION

I am not a product of my circumstances. I am a product of my decisions.
—Stephen Covey, educator and author

The internal transition, which results in making the commitment to switch ladders, is only the beginning—a big beginning. This sets up the procedure for the practical, external steps we need to take.

Here's one important caution for those of us who decide to switch ladders: Don't leave badly. We don't want to make enemies or hurt feelings when we leave. We need to leave a door open so that we can go back. You don't plan to go back, but you never know if you'll need something from them in the future.

I never expected to return, but I have no way of knowing the future. What if I were mistaken? What if, two years later, I wanted to have some kind of association with them? Or what if I wanted to use their facilities for meetings? Or if I needed recommendations from them.

Too many resign and carry bad feelings toward others. They use those last days as opportunities to vent their anger or dissatisfaction. I offer one word of advice: Don't.

If there are issues, we need to resolve them first or hold them until we're gone. That also means that the resignation letter needs to be thought through carefully with no venting. This is just as true regarding any public speaking opportunity.

Too often, CEOs and pastors leave and decide that, as long as they're leaving, they will take their parting shots at everyone. Instead of facing the individuals with whom they had difficulties, they take the passive/aggressive pathway and vent grievances before everyone.

In my case, as I wrote my letter of resignation, there was nothing to vent about, because I had been treated well, loved the people I worked with and felt an immense amount of gratitude to God for the years I had been the president.

When we leave, we want to have a genuine smile on our face, warmth in our heart and hear no angry noises behind us.

In my case, I didn't want anyone to think I was jumping off a sinking ship or that I had some information that we were in decline. More than once, I made it clear that nothing was wrong, I wasn't going to a rival school, and I had no dissatisfactions. I wasn't trying to say that life was perfect, but my relationship with everyone—so far as I knew—had been excellent.

My years as the head of the school also enabled me to have the kind of public platform I have today. Had I remained the pastor of a congregation, I would have had a ministry, but not nearly as wide as the one God gave me through my association with the college. They were wonderful, exciting years, but it was time to bring them to a close. I had to leave because God had new doors waiting for me to open and walk through.

Our exit strategy is more important than our entrance. That is, how we leave is more important than how we came in. When CEOs or pastors discuss leaving with me, I ask, "What will you be remembered for?"

I tell them about my resigning from the college. When I became president in 1989, we had only eighty-seven students. When I left on December 31, 2003, we had 690. The point, however, is that none of the students from 1989 were still there. None of those students who welcomed me would be there when I left. So, I asked, How would I be remembered? How did I want to be remembered?

The answer seemed obvious: I want to be remembered for how I left rather than how I came in. We can all tell stories of leaders who came in to change things, and everyone rallied behind them. They used words such as "greatest" or "biggest" or "most spiritual," but they didn't last. As the old saying goes, "They came in with a roar and went out with a whimper."

People remember our departure, and they tell others. Many pastors left good churches, and CEOs left good organizations, but they departed in such a way that their reception at the next place was tainted. Word does get around.

We must never forget that we live in a very small world. People talk to people. News has a way of traveling. Wherever we land next, information about how we left the previous place follows. This is especially true if the new employer starts a background check.

When any leader leaves and parts with harsh words, bitterness, fractured relationships or in a passive-aggressive manner, there is nothing to celebrate. If there is celebration for their leaving at a farewell, it's either perfunctory or a sense of, "At least he's leaving."

Instead, we need to do everything we can to make peace and to mend bad relationships—as much as it depends on us. Thus, how we leave is more critical than how we arrive.

My most difficult task in leaving, however—and I assume this is true of all leaders—is to give up control. Once leaders say, "I'm leaving," power and control are out of their hands. They can't determine the future or the decisions others will make. I did the best I could.

Someone went before me; someone will come after me. I can serve with my utmost commitment where I am right now; I can also look ahead and prepare the rungs for my successor to climb.

Not everyone can focus on the future. Some are too insecure and not even sure they can stay on the ladder themselves, but wise, secure leaders plan for their succession the day they start the job. We can do great service for our organizations if we start the process early. We can't always pick our successors, but we can create a healthy environment for their arrival. No matter what our leadership role, we can begin to shape the profile of the next person to follow.

I looked ahead to ask what problems my departure could cause my successor. What issues do I need to deal with while I still can do something about them? John Maxwell gave me this advice: "In the last few months, ask yourself, What can I do now that will help the next man?"

He said that he cleaned house. There were people who needed to go. He didn't want his successor to have his problems because he was the one who hired those people. I did that for my successor in great part. I released those who weren't carrying their loads. It wasn't easy, but I believe I did the right thing.

There is one other issue—that of being a lame duck. How do we to stay productive during the lame-duck period? This was a big issue for me to cope with. I had resigned in the middle of October, and I would have two-and-a-half months left at the school. The good thing is the college closed for Thanksgiving week, and after the second week of December students would be gone, so it was down time. In my research, I discovered that almost all college presidents announced their resignation long in advance and actually resigned

June 30, because the fiscal year for all colleges begins in July, and they had no down time. That's one of the reasons why I timed it as I did.

I didn't want to be a lame duck for too long—not just for their sake but for my sake. I had mentally packed my bags, and my heart was no longer at the school. It wasn't fair to them for me to stay.

CHAPTER 20
THE LADDER TO LEGACY

What you leave behind is not what is engraved in stone monuments, but what is woven into the lives of others.
—Pericles, Greek statesman

The actions we take during the first three months while we ascend our new ladders largely determine whether we succeed or fail. If we fumble during that time, we may be able to make up for it—but it won't be easy. We need to make the most of transitions—especially in those first three months.

Transitions provide unique opportunities—chances to start afresh and make needed changes. Almost every leader knows that. What they often don't consider is that those first ninety days are also a period of acute vulnerability. During that period, they will establish working relationships and will define their roles.

In any job, there is something called "paying the rent." Those are the things that we absolutely must do. If I'm a pastor, I must preach

Sundays, conduct baptisms and funerals, officiate at weddings and moderate at board meetings. Thirty years ago, researchers figured that "paying the rent" is a half-time job. A large part of the leader's mark (legacy) depends on what they do the other half of their work week. For pastors, some teach classes. Others engage in political activities; some build programs or focus on evangelism. What they do after paying the rent is as important as the effectiveness with which they work.

In his book, *The First 90 Days: Critical Success Strategies for New Leaders at All Levels*, Michael Watkins, associate professor of the Harvard Business School, refers to the "breakeven point." That is when new leaders have contributed as much value to their new organization as they have consumed from it. He also offers ten suggestions to face the transition challenges:

- Make a definite, final, mental break from your old job.

- Accelerate your learning.

- Match strategy to situation. (A clear diagnosis of the situation is essential.)

- Secure early wins to build credibility and create momentum.

- Negotiate success with your boss by managing expectations.

- Achieve alignment between organizational structure and its strategy.

- Build or restructure your team.

- Create coalitions or supportive alliances.

- Keep your balance and your ability to make good judgments. (The risk of losing perspective and making bad calls is ever present during transitions.)

- Help everyone in your organization to accelerate their own transitions and strengthen succession planning (leadership transition acceleration).

In the same way that the first three months of our new assignment establish patterns for long-term success in our roles, the final months of our tenure can have an outsized impact on our legacy. As I have noted earlier, we must strive to finish well and finish strong, as our departures will shape how we are remembered and may even atone for some of the mistakes we will have inevitably made in the course of our time as leaders.

When I started to think about what I was leaving, one of the first things I thought about was my legacy. Over the years, I've visited churches and companies where they have a gallery of pictures of their past leaders. They rarely show anything except a picture of the person and the years they served.

I know one church that does it differently. It has existed since 1853. Although it's in a fairly small city, and the church never had a membership larger than 350, the congregations have done one significant thing to honor the legacy of their leaders. Under each picture, in three or four paragraphs, they list that pastor's achievements. The first pastor had founded the church because he believed in freeing slaves. Members had pledged themselves to actively support emancipation. Three pictures from the end is a red-headed minister who had volunteered as a chaplain in 1942—only weeks after World War II had begun. He died in the Normandy invasion in 1944.

That's the way organizations need to work. Instead of denying or burying evidence of those who led, those who follow need to appreciate their legacies.

I began thinking about my legacy. *What am I leaving behind?* I asked myself. I didn't know if anyone would even remember my name thirty years from then. That wasn't my point. I wanted to leave a legacy that shaped the future of the school. Whether I received credit in the long run wasn't important. It was important that I left with a sense of accomplishment behind me.

Some days I paused and thought, *I've been more blessed than any human being can imagine.* I had come to the United States as a foreigner whose English was sometimes difficult to apprehend—who didn't understand many American customs or expressions—and God had given (and still does give) me such great favor. Even though I knew it was time to leave, and my zeal had waned, my gratitude had not.

One day I said aloud to myself, "The kind of legacy I want to leave is a mark on human hearts."

I realized that I wanted to know there would be those who would say things such as, "Without the influence of Sam Chand, I wouldn't have made it." "Sam believed in me, and I learned to believe in myself." "I wanted to work for God, but I had no idea what it was. Sam helped me see my potential. God used him to take me where I am today."

Because of that yearning for a human legacy, the urge became even stronger to move from behind the desk to sit across from people.

I also wondered, *Can I live without my present professional identity? Will my influence be limited? Will it continue or diminish?*

While I was president, I could pick up the phone, and I was two calls away from any leader. I didn't know if that would continue. My identity had been that of president of the college. Before I became president, we used to say that the college was one of the nation's best-kept secrets. But now, at least in certain circles, it is recognized as a forward-thinking institution and has proven invaluable to the community.

What am I giving up along with that position? Will people return my phone calls? Will they continue to recognize me? Now that I can't do something for them as I had before, will I still be significant in their lives?

Here's another question: *Have I been significant to people because of who I am or for what I do?* Most of us are afraid to ask ourselves that because the truth says, "It's because of what I do."

I had fearful feelings of walking away from everything I'd worked for and built up. At the college, there was not one square inch of that entire property that remained the same. That wasn't easy to leave, because brick and mortar have a way of defining us. This was my house. It placed me. I had somewhere to take people that was physical and tangible. And then it was gone. Now what?

I asked myself to suppose I was just a Christian who came into a church, sat in the back row every Sunday for four months. Then I missed three Sundays in a row. Who would call me? Would anyone e-mail or write to me? Would anyone care if I weren't there?

The answer is that nobody would call and nobody would care. However, if I missed one Sunday as pastor, of course, everybody would want to know what was wrong. It was easy to see my worth because I was on the payroll and employed by the church. If that's all there was, when I'm no longer there, does that mean I'm nothing?

It does unless I have grasped that my real value is internal and not just what I do for others.

When people talk about how important I am, I often smile and say, "Let me tell you what the conversation will be fifteen minutes after my funeral. The questions will go along this line: 'Where's the potato salad? What happened to all the beans?'"

I may have said it lightly, but I didn't take it lightly. When we leave a position of leadership—senior elder, CEO, vice-president or pastor— we leave something behind. Ask pastors' widows; they know. They were the center of the church life one month, and the next they were pushed to the side. Of course, they were no longer the pastors' wives, but too often, they become people without identity.

I didn't want to leave the college without a sense of identity or feeling I had left the best part of myself behind. I wanted to leave with the idea that I was enhancing my identity and my sense of self-worth.

Will the organization be able to sustain what I have started? Who and what is the organization going to lose because of my exit? Like a pastor who receives a call to a different congregation, I had to ask, "If I leave, who else will leave? Who will the school lose?"

I think that's more true for non-profit organizations than for-profit corporations. And yet in many large corporations when the top person leaves, there is often a big shake-up. In 2004, it happened with the Coca-Cola Company in Atlanta. One of its major vice presidents left because the board had bypassed him and not selected him as the next president.

In many churches, when the senior pastor leaves, a lot of staff leave. In some denominations such as the Assemblies of God, after the senior pastor leaves and a new pastor comes in, everyone on staff resigns. The new leader doesn't have to accept the resignations, but at least they're there and provide an opportunity to make changes.

What am I leaving behind? In answering that question, I also realized the importance of relationships that I would leave behind. No matter how much I liked some of the people I worked with, my moving would mean they would have to change. Some people can push them away because there is always someone else to relate to. I value those long-term relationships. I had developed a number of them and wanted to maintain them. I also realized that some of them would have to be on a different level.

CONCLUSION

If we're observant, we'll notice that God has fashioned our lives to follow patterns. In the natural world, these patterns are known as seasons. The sage of Ecclesiastes wrote, "There is a time for everything, and a season for every activity under the heavens" (Ecclesiastes 3:1, NIV).

Like the seasons that reflect the birth, growth, productivity and end of life on earth, the seasons of our lives cannot be rigidly calculated. Some winters are long and snowy. Some springs are "unseasonably" warm. No one can determine the day the first snowflake will fall or the moment the first bud will emerge. Even so, we take comfort in the predictability of the seasons and the changes that each one brings.

Likewise, while each person's journey is unique, there are seasons marked by key decisions, moments of crisis or opportunity, developmental milestones and other major events—each one occurring at somewhat different points for different people.

I believe there are four of these seasons that we experience, and each one is characterized by unique events—some of which happen to us without our ability to change them, and others that require our direct involvement as we transition from one season to the next.

In our *Starting* season (from birth to about age 20), we are shaped by our families of origin, birthplace, gender and physical makeup. While we have little control over many of the factors, we carry their impact throughout our lives. Arguably, our leadership potential in adulthood is influenced by questions that are asked in this stage, such as those of self-worth ("Do I matter?"), confidence ("Am I able?") and destiny and purpose ("Why was I placed on this earth?"). This is why we often see the seeds of leadership in children on a playground who may be decades away from a seat in the corner office.

In our *Searching* season (ages 20 to 40), we are completing our education, getting married or starting a family, finding our job and developing competence in a field. Looking at the "ladder" metaphor that has shaped this book, it is in this season that we are growing in the skills addressed in Part II. We may have many jobs as we find the sweet spot of calling and vocation, all along identifying strengths and weaknesses, preferences and styles, gravitating toward some leaders as mentors and holding ladders for others.

In our *Success* season (ages 40 to 55), we are merging the competencies of our Searching season with our gifts, role and influence. We move from the "doing" characteristic of the Searching season to "being." We are secure in our roles and gaining the respect of those whose ladders we hold and those who are holding ours. We may also find great comfort in our positions and become risk averse. It is often in this season that we will face a critical incident that will cause disruption from without, or a sense of godly discontent that will move us from within. When this happens, we must have the courage to step off our current ladder to a new and unfamiliar one.

In our *Significance* season (ages 50 and older), our focus is convergence, legacy and destiny. To put it bluntly, we begin to get concerned about what will be written on our tombstone, how we will be remembered and whether the impact of our life and leadership will outlive us. We will face the challenges of succession addressed in Part III of this book, and in order to expand our influence, we may be called to release our leadership—a painful yet liberating experience.

In each of these seasons, bold moves will be required of us. For some moves, we will need to climb a ladder, step down from one or move to another ladder. But each one will demand our courage. While this book has addressed many of the practical nuts and bolts of developing ladder holders, growing in the skills needed to climb and making the ladder transitions, when the time comes, I want to leave you with three of the essentials that I believe are necessary for making your next bold move.

First, you must have a *dream*. This must be *your* dream, not one given you by a parent, spouse or boss. As a dream releaser, this is something I'm passionate about. However, I realize that it is not my dreams that are being released, but the dreams of those I am helping. While a dream may be influenced by external circumstances, ultimately, it takes root in your own heart and is the culmination of myriad personal desires and divine interventions.

You may be tempted to share your dream far and wide—after all, it is inspiring and invigorating. But I would caution you to take your time. Don't share your dream too soon, and be careful with whom you share it. Instead, allow it to percolate, develop and refine itself. Your next bold move will be the natural outflow of your dream. If it's not, you may need to reevaluate the move itself, as the two should align.

If you are a naturally conservative person, you may be tempted to exercise caution or risk aversion in dreaming. The vagaries and circumstances of life will naturally whittle down your dream, but you should not be the one to do so. Dream big, God-sized dreams. Let Him adjust your expectations, if need be, but don't hesitate to explore possibilities that will only come to fruition with His intervention.

Second, you will need *determination*. You should expect resistance. In fact, if you face no resistance, you should probably reevaluate a move that seems too easy to be true or too simple to engender doubt. A bold move is one that will require your complete attention, your undying perseverance and your willingness to approach an unknown future without certainty of success. You will be tempted to quit, but the only thing worse than a quitter is someone who never begins.

Finally, you'll need a *developer*. As I shared earlier in the book, one of my regrets is that I never had someone mentoring me during several of my bold moves. Would the outcome have been different? I'll never know, but I know that your journey will be enhanced by the presence of mentors. A mentor is someone who is committed to you as a person, to your life journey and to your ultimate purpose. It is through this grid that they are able to actively listen and offer insight, when needed.

As you make your next bold move, you can have great confidence that the God who shaped you for His purposes is watching over each transition of your life. As the psalmist notes,

> *The Lord will keep you from all harm—*
> *he will watch over your life;*
> *the Lord will watch over your coming and going*
> *both now and forevermore.*
> —Psalm 121:7-8 (NIV)

INSPIRE

IMPACT CULTURE, INFLUENCE CHANGE

INTRODUCING THE INSPIRE COLLECTIVE

While many churches are effective in equipping Christians for ministry within their walls, some struggle to prepare them for service in other arenas—their workplace, their neighborhood, their social community.

But the call to be change-makers is for all believers: Artists, business people, civic servants, community leaders, educators, mechanics, stay-at-home parents, students, and wait-staff.

That's why the Inspire Collective was established, to help raise up true influencers who are kingdom-focused Monday through Saturday, not just on Sundays.

The Inspire Collective delivers a unique blend of inspiration and application, spiritual and practical, for those wanting to impact and influence their everyday world for Christ.

THE INSPIRE COLLECTIVE OFFERS

- MAGAZINE
- BOOKS
- STUDY RESOURCES
- COURSES
- LIVE CLASSES
- EVENTS
- LOCAL NETWORKS

FOUNDED BY
Mike Kai, Martijn van Tilborgh, Sam Chand

INSPIRECOLLECTIVE.COM